I AM A PROTESTANT

I AM A PROTESTANT

BY

RAY FREEMAN JENNEY

THE BOBBS-MERRILL COMPANY, INC.

INDIANAPOLIS　　*Publishers*　　NEW YORK

COPYRIGHT, 1951, BY THE BOBBS-MERRILL COMPANY, INC.

PRINTED IN THE UNITED STATES OF AMERICA

BY THE HADDON CRAFTSMEN, SCRANTON, PA.

284
J54

Dever

1.50

17 Nov. 67

28161

This book is dedicated to my wife, a Protestant,
who day by day bears witness in word and deed
and truth to the Christian faith.

TABLE OF CONTENTS

TABLE OF CONTENTS

I AM A PROTESTANT

Preface

WHY THIS BOOK

THIS book is primarily for the laymen of the Protestant faith. It is neither an attack on the Roman Catholic Church nor a defense of the Protestant Church. It is a pro-Protestant pronouncement.

An attempt has been made to write this book in a plain, comprehensible way in order that the reader may understand the heritage, basic teachings and cardinal principles of Protestant Christianity. In the attempt to put ideas into clear language it is hoped that scholarship has not been neglected.

The reasons for this book are obvious. Most theologians write for other theologians, using terms which are not readily understood by the average layman. Their work is often obscure even to the clergymen who read their books, perhaps in part because they are harassed by their fellow ministers who ask, "Have you read So and So's book?" One of the functions of a helpful clergyman is to interpret the scholars. His primary task is to instruct the people in his church in the faith they profess and make portable in understanding terms the fresh and helpful ideas of the good and thoughtful men of every age.

Those who work with young people in colleges and universities, and the Protestant chaplains in both World Wars I and II, report that Roman Catholic young people are better indoctrinated in the teachings of their Church and their relationship to it, than are the Protestant young people, most of whom are vague about Christian doctrine and why they are Protestants. This book is written to help correct this grievous difference. The endeavor has been made to give a sense of what is distinctive in our Protestant faith, also to diagnose the weakness and strength of our Church and to prescribe a cure.

It is evident that the Roman Catholic Church is conducting a strenuous campaign with both an immediate and a long-range plan to make America Catholic. Under the Constitution of our country the Roman Catholics have a perfect right to propagate and proselyte for the Catholic faith. No one can deny them that right or justly claim that the Roman Catholic Church is bigoted when she exerts every effort to carry to a successful conclusion her plan and purpose.

The Protestant Church must exercise that same right, with "zeal plus knowledge" and do it with a wise statesmanship which is largely lacking today. Too long have the Protestants been divided into three camps: the bigots, who think with their emotions and claim they have a monopoly on truth; those who are so tolerant and broad-minded that they have no definite convictions and are a positive menace to their Church; and those who are increasingly aware of the dangers of Roman Catholic domination in America, and resolve to be pro-Protestant. The urgent need is to make the Protestant Church strong, effective and dominant for the well-being of all.

It is a hopeful sign that there is an increasing number of Protestant Church members, both lay and clergy, who support this third position. Particularly is this true of the able lay people. It is the intelligently concerned Protestant clergy and lay people who are "the last best hope" of America. They are the ones who will help give democracy a chance to demonstrate its value. Better yet, they will help men to exercise their right of private judgment and to further the rule and reign of God as a redemptive force.

In this book an honest attempt has been made to awaken Protestants to an intelligent appreciation of their splendid heritage and motivate them to do their part to extend and improve the Protestant method, spirit and purpose throughout

the world. Living effectively as a Protestant will require believing men and women to take a position once again and
learn to hold that position unswervingly. We must face the
weaknesses in the Protestant faith, and after we confess our
sins then we can confer with one another and seek a cure for
our ills. It is later than we think, and unless we Protestants
are "stabbed broad awake," and at once begin to assume our
responsibility and assert our rights, ecclesiastical as well as
political dictatorship will be imposed upon us. We shall be
responsible for that condition because we did not use aright
the talent God entrusted to us. We must use our talent or
lose it.

It is my desire to go back to the roots of our religion, for
I contend that Protestant Christianity can be understood only
as it is grounded in definite historical events. Yet we must
not be imprisoned by the past. Chapters II, III and VII will
serve as a concise handbook for the layman who desires to
know the why, how and what of his faith and to the clergyman who is not so wise but that he, too, would be eager to
understand better the ABC's of his faith.

Chapters II and III give a thumbnail sketch of the Reformers. Particular attention is given to Luther, Calvin and Knox.
It is imperative to gain an understanding of others who were
forerunners of the Reformation of the sixteenth century, and
of those who came after them in the continuing Reformation.
Consideration is given in Chapter VII to the various ways the
Protestant Church has sought to achieve unity and effectiveness.

The beliefs which set aflame the souls of the early disciples
and of the Reformers are the dynamic and imperative needs
of our day. It is vitally important that you and I become
grounded in those beliefs, that we reinterpret them afresh for
our day, and that you and I reaffirm them.

The ideas in this book have been presented by me in various

ways—in sermons, lectures, forums, classes in Christian citizenship—in my thirty years in the ministry. I have ever sought to keep from furthering hatred among my people, from aiding and increasing bigotry and from making my people anti-Catholic in the narrow sense of the term. Moreover, I have endeavored by word and deed to awaken the Protestant laymen and ministers to be pro-Protestant. That is both one's right and one's duty!

This book has come out of a dual interest. First, I have a love of church history. It was my good fortune to have as my teacher Dr. Arthur Cushman McGiffert of Union Theological Seminary, an internationally recognized historian, who inspired his students with a love of history. Second, I have an equally keen interest in theology, i.e., the science of God. God is not thought of as some far-off Olympian deity aloof from the world, but a God of all people, who cares and counts in the affairs of men; a God of justice, love and mercy, as revealed by Jesus Christ, whom the world needs to know if it would be saved from destruction.

You and I need to ask humbly, honestly and earnestly, "What shall we do with Jesus' teachings, his life, his death and his resurrection?" Mine is a faith that humbly tries to understand the mind and purpose of Christ and to take him in earnest. It is my desire to share and extend this faith.

I have sought in this book to speak boldly and to state my views frankly without resort to either diatribes or dogmatic conclusions. Earnestly have I endeavored never to allow my convictions to undermine judgment, lure me to intolerant denunciations or divert me from being Christian in my attitude.

In these fearful days, a vivid and vital interpretation of great truths in new forms is needed, those truths by which men can act as free men in the most real sense. These are crucial days and I believe that the well-being and hope of the world are dependent on free men who are socially minded and who are spiritually motivated.

The basic aim of all Protestant Christians is found in the Great Commandment of Jesus (Matthew 22:37-39), which according to King James Version reads: "Thou shalt love the Lord thy God with all thy heart, and with all thy soul, and with all thy mind. . . . Thou shalt love thy neighbour as thyself." This is my faith! I have seen this faith verified. You and I can and must verify it again and again. This is why I am constrained to write this book.

I wish to acknowledge my debt to the many authors who, down through the years, have contributed to my thinking on this subject. The stimulation afforded by their insights has made possible whatever clarity and conviction my own position may possess.

RAY FREEMAN JENNEY

1

WHY WE ARE PROTESTANTS

PERIODICALLY the Pope issues an invitation to all Protestants to unite with the Roman Catholic Church. Recently such an invitation was given. While it was not sent to me personally, its purpose was to have every individual Protestant consider it as a personal one and accept it. Therefore, I have given this invitation careful and prayerful consideration.

This response is presented in the most friendly spirit. We should remember that "enemies should be cautious but friends should be frank." Christians should ever seek for the spirit of reconciliation. Faber's hymn, "There's a Wideness in God's Mercy," is apt here:

> There's a wideness in God's mercy,
> Like the wideness of the sea;
> There's a kindness in His justice,
> Which is more than liberty.

> For the love of God is broader
> Than the measures of man's mind,
> And the heart of the Eternal
> Is most wonderfully kind.

"Why am I a Protestant?" For a majority of people the answer is "Because my parents were Protestants." You and I were born into Protestant homes. If we had been born into

Roman Catholic homes we would have, no doubt, been Roman Catholics. The faith of our fathers is our faith. Yet that is only a partial answer. In a day when one may think for himself and get facts if he desires them, a person need not stay the way he was born, pledged forever to tradition.

Yet if we go back a little over four hundred years, we find that our ancestors were largely Roman Catholics. Some do not need to go back that far. Our forefathers became Protestant because of a deep conviction that the faith their fathers had was unsatisfactory for them and that they must have a faith of their own which they could respect. The Roman Church was renounced as being unsound in principle and practice according to New Testament standards.

American Protestantism is confronted with a challenge such as it has never met before, one which compels us to think clearly and speak vigorously. Throughout the latter part of the eighteenth century and all of the nineteenth the Protestant churches worked together to create a political framework in America, in which Roman Catholics should feel equally at home. Now in this twentieth century the Roman Catholic hierarchy is telling us that they alone are the divinely appointed Church; that the state should favor them as such; that we Protestants are purveyors of error and consequently should not be given equal status with champions of truth.

Today, we are in danger of losing not only our civil freedom, but our religious freedom as well. In order to cope with this fact, we need a fresh understanding of the sixteenth-century Reformation and a recognition of the value of a continuing Reformation. Some contend that we are now in a re-reformation age. If further reformation is necessary, then we Protestants should be informed and clear-sighted about the basic problems that must be solved if life is to have real meaning and our religious faith is to be vital. Too frequently a Protestant is a non-Catholic in the same sense that a Gentile

is a non-Jew. But to be a Protestant in fact should mean that
a person has certain definite beliefs, stands for certain basic
truths and clings to them just as zealously as a Catholic clings
to those beliefs and ideas which make him a Roman Catholic.
Beliefs which one has taken for granted must be traced back
to their true meaning and made as applicable to this century
as they were to the sixteenth century. The Protestant must
understand the reasons for the faith within him, the faith that
he professes.

> Before I built a wall, I'd ask to know
> What I was walling in or walling out . . .
> Something there is that doesn't love a wall,
> That wants it down.[1]

So Robert Frost, the New Hampshire poet, puts these
words on the tongue of an old New England farmer who
every spring rebuilds the walls which needlessly divide two
neighboring orchards.

It is perhaps true that Protestants know more about what
they want to "wall out" than they do about what they want
to "wall in." Actually we Protestants know all too well why
we are not Roman Catholics, but we are rather poorly informed as to why we are Protestants. If we look at the facts,
where will they take us? Back into the Roman Catholic
Church? Or toward a concerned and stalwart Protestantism?
These questions are not only personal but are of national,
even world-wide importance. The historical connection between Protestantism and democracy is essential for the well-
being of both the Church and democracy.

Many thoughtful men and women in the Protestant Church
have become increasingly disturbed, even alarmed, about Ro-

---

[1] From *Complete Poems of Robert Frost, 1949.* Copyright, 1930, 1949, by
Henry Holt and Company, Inc. Reprinted by permission of the publisher.

man Catholicism and its attitude of absolute authority. In the light of these events it is our duty to re-evaluate our Protestant heritage of faith. Is there just cause for alarm? What has Protestantism to offer? These questions should be considered objectively, without fear or favor. Yet we should earnestly strive to be positive and constructive. Anyone who is guilty of feeding the fires of intolerance or of increasing the spirit of religious prejudice or bigotry in our day has committed a crime against mankind. He has rendered a real disservice to the Christian Church as well.

Our future is precarious because of pagan forces in the world which are attempting to overthrow all religion completely. Among them are nationalism, materialism and secularism which tend to make religion a mouthpiece of leaders, or if possible, to extirpate it.

In such a threatening world situation as ours, all who believe in Christ and his teachings ought to be united against common relentless enemies who seek our downfall rather than to be fighting each other on account of differences in the expression of our religious beliefs. We should come to a broad understanding that "we agree to differ" in theology and polity, but resolve to work each in his own way and with God for the advancement of the kingdom of God in the heart and mind of every individual everywhere.

"When Roman Catholics will not work with us, what are we Protestants to do?" This is a question many of us ask. The reasons why we should endeavor to work together are not superficial, but on the contrary, very important. Both Protestants and Catholics are interpreters of the same gospel as revealed in Jesus Christ. They have a common God, a common Christ, a common Cross and in large part a common Bible.

Dr. W. Russell Bowie, whom Catholics acknowledge as

"one of the most scholarly and influential Protestant clergymen in the United States" has said:

Protestants can sincerely admire the steadfastness in which,
in the midst of contemporary secularism and shallow thinking, Roman Catholicism bears its constant witness to a higher
world of which every man must alone be a citizen if his soul
is not to shrivel. We can recognize the massive dignity of an
organized life and worship rich with the traditions of many
centuries, and the worth of a fellowship which reaches round
the world and includes communicants of every nation and
race. We can honor the heroic devotion of many Roman
Catholic priests and missionaries, the life-long and unreserved
dedication to God and service in religious orders both of
monks and nuns, and ideals of saintliness which have been
lifted up and to which the greater souls in generation after
generation have aspired.[2]

Three major movements are in competition for ascendancy
in the spiritual and cultural life of this country: Protestantism,
Catholicism and Secularism. Some able students in the field
of religion contend that if Protestantism continues in its sectarian inertia, America's culture is destined to be either secular
or Roman Catholic.

As Protestant Christians we believe in the dignity and
worth of all human beings. We also believe in the freedom
and right of individuals to be guided by conscience, and that
each individual is accountable directly to God. We further
affirm that our religious belief is founded on a knowledge of
what we believe and we have reasons with which we can defend our beliefs. It is then that we have an established faith
in God.

The Catholic, contrary to this, is dominated by a kind of

---

[2] W. Russell Bowie, "Protestant Concern over Catholicism," *The American
Mercury* (September 1949), pp. 261, 262.

religion, so organized that he is a victim of a faith bound up in relentless assumptions and handed out to him with little right or freedom on his part to think for himself.

We as Protestants do not want any ecclesiastical dictatorship, nor do we want political dictatorship. We believe firmly in the separation of the Church and the State. We recognize the Roman Church as totalitarian in philosophy, theology and practice; therefore, as Protestants we are concerned and disturbed, if we are thoughtful, because we, as Dr. Bowie has further said, "are obliged to believe that the clearly stated Roman Catholic purpose 'to make America Catholic,' if it succeeded would jeopardize the religious and civil liberties which have been the glory of Protestant countries and Protestant culture."[3] It is therefore our duty as Protestant Christians to see to it that the Roman Catholic Church shall not as a totalitarian autocracy dominate our civil and our religious life.

It may be contended by some that these are hard words born out of ignorance, intolerance and bigotry, that anyone who utters them is anti-Catholic. To me personally, this label does not apply, in general or in any bill of particulars. A careful and honest examination of my record in thirty years of the ministry will prove my statement. I have consistently leaned over backward to be friendly and co-operative with my Roman Catholic friends and to try to understand the position of the Roman Catholic Church. I can justly claim to have a comprehensive understanding of church history, both Catholic and Protestant. I have had and now have many dear and honored friends in both the priesthood and laity of the Catholic Church. Among them I number the late Bishop John A. Duffy, of the Diocese of Buffalo; Monsignor George A. Parker, of St. Philip Neri Church, Father Edward V. Cardi-

---

[3] *Ibid.*, p. 262.

nal, Director, Sheil School Catholic Youth Organization, and
Mayor Martin H. Kennelly, all of Chicago.

For years I have served faithfully on interfaith committees and movements, and have sought constantly for understanding and reconciliation among Protestants and Roman
Catholics and Jews; but so often I have sought in vain for
fellowship with the Roman Catholics because of an unyield-
ing self-sufficiency on the part of the majority of the priesthood of that Church. In the eyes of a majority of Roman
Catholics, all Protestants are anti-Catholic if they do not take
every utterance made by that Church as truth. In the eyes
of an unbiased judge our only crime is that we are pro-Protestant. To that charge I personally, quickly and gladly, plead
guilty. Every man should be loyal to his own faith. Like
Martin Luther each one of us must say, without dealing in
heroics, what he is popularly reported to have said: "Here I
stand. I cannot do otherwise. God help me." We need to
hear and heed Paul's words in Galatians: "Stand fast therefore in the liberty wherewith Christ hath made us free, and
be not entangled again with the yoke of bondage." Our minds
and hearts and souls should respond in glad loyalty to that
clarion call.

To stand up for Protestantism is not at all synonymous
with standing against Romanism. Again I say, one ought to
be constructively and intelligently loyal to one's faith. A true
Protestant should stand against totalitarianism in every form,
economic, political and ecclesiastical. Furthermore, he should
stand for the liberty of mind and spirit which is the guarantee
of truth and freedom for all. We do not want political dictatorship; neither do we want ecclesiastical dictatorship. This
I reiterate, for it is a basic truth.

There is evidence in abundance in countries such as Italy,
Spain and Mexico that the Roman Catholic Church controls
education, the laws concerning marriage and divorce, and all

moral regulations for all the people without regard to whether or not they belong to the Catholic Church. It imposes on the minority groups such regulation and limitations that it makes it difficult, if not impossible, for any other religious faith to operate in a country where the Roman Catholic Church is in a majority.

The Protestants who live in America are prone to say "It can't happen here," yet they know that it might happen here, if they understand the philosophy of the Roman Catholic Church as recorded by Paul Blanshard in his well-documented book:

The Roman Catholic Church, convinced, through its divine prerogatives, of being the only true church, must demand the right of freedom for herself alone, because such a right can only be possessed by truth, never by error. As to other religions, the Church will certainly never draw the sword, but she will require that by legitimate means they shall not be allowed to propagate false doctrine. Consequently, in a state where the majority of the people are Catholic, the Church will require that legal existence be denied to error, and that if religious minorities actually exist, they shall have only a *de facto* existence without opportunity to spread their beliefs. . . . In some countries, Catholics will be obliged to ask full religious freedom for all, resigned at being forced to cohabitate where they alone should rightfully be allowed to live. But in doing this the Church does not renounce her thesis, which remains the most imperative of her laws, but merely adapts herself to *de facto* conditions, which must be taken into account in practical affairs. . . . The Church cannot blush for her own want of tolerance, as she asserts it in principle and applies it in practice.[4]

Thus we perceive that the Roman Catholic Church, through representatives of the Vatican and by constant pressure of her

-----

4 From *Cività Cattolica* (Rome, April 1948), quoted in *American Freedom and Catholic Power*, by Paul Blanshard (Boston, The Beacon Press, 1949), p. 295. Reprinted by permission of the publishers.

priesthood, does endeavor with vigilance to instruct her own communicants, but also that she tries to force her teaching and restrictions on all people. The Roman Catholic Church may not "blush for her own want of tolerance," but she surely should blush for her arrogance.

The ruler of the Church, the Pope, claims sovereignty by divine right, and he is also the head of a small state, the Vatican State, created by the Lateran Treaty of 1929 with Mussolini. This Vatican State is ruled by the same machinery that rules the religious aspects of the Church. "The Holy Father is not alone the supreme head of the Catholic Church. He is also the head of a sovereign State. Thirty-eight countries have representatives at the Holy See."[5]

In the same Lateran Treaty it was provided that "the Roman Catholic Apostolic religion is the sole religion of the State."

Louis Veuillot, a French Catholic writer, has stated tersely and emphatically the same paradoxical principle underlying the Roman Catholic thought and work. He said, "When we are in a minority, we ask religious liberty in the name of your (Protestant) principles. When we are in a majority, we refuse it in the name of ours."[6] This is an attitude which cannot be overlooked and against which Protestants should take a positive and concerted stand.

In the Federal Council's Information Service of October 29, 1949, there was a summarization of facts which had been gleaned from various sources in regard to the denial of religious liberty in Spain. In the *Federal Council Bulletin* of September 1950 it was reported that official confirmation of

---

[5] *American Freedom and Catholic Power*, pp. 40, 41.

[6] From A. Stewart McNairn's "Freedom as Interpreted by Rome" (*World Dominion and the World Today*, London, July-August 1943), quoted in George P. Howard, *Religious Liberty in South America* (Philadelphia, the Westminster Press, 1944), p. 18. Reprinted by permission of the publisher.

these facts had been received from the Spanish government. The *Bulletin* further reported:

In response to a plea for religious liberty presented to General Franco by representatives of Spanish Protestants, the head of the Spanish cabinet referred them to a letter of instruction which had been sent to all provincial governors in February 1948, although not made public at that time.

This letter of instruction is an authoritative interpretation of "religious liberty" as conceived by the Spanish government. It makes it clear that the Sixth Article of the Spanish Charter as thus interpreted, which seems superficially to assure a measure of religious liberty, actually denies any religious liberty worthy of the name.

Article VI declares that "no one shall be molested for his religious beliefs or the private practice of worship." The interpretation which is not made public undertakes to define "the private practice of worship," as distinguished from "abuses and infringements" of the same. This worship, it is declared:

may in no case have outward or public manifestations, on the one hand because then it would no longer be private, which is the unique form in which it is allowed, and on the other hand because the only outward manifestations and ceremonies which are permitted are those of the Catholic religion.

The official interpretation bluntly concludes:

Consequently, there is no place for the practice of any act of proselytism or propaganda whatsoever by the non-Catholic religions, whatever may be the method used, as, for instance, the founding of educational institutions, gifts having the appearance of philanthropy, recreational centers, etc., for this would necessarily involve an outward manifestation, which is not permitted.

In a word, there is no liberty in Spain for those outside the Roman Catholic Church to carry on any kind of evangelistic or educational or social work whatsoever. Yet we had been asked to believe that the Spanish Constitution assured religious liberty.

It is heartening to know that there is an awareness on the part of the Roman Catholics over the suppression, in countries where the Roman Church is dominant, of the freedom that it claims for itself in countries in which it is relatively weak.

Father John Courtney Murray, the American Jesuit scholar who edits *Theological Studies,* is one of the representatives of the new trend. Among the European scholars cited with approval by Father Murray (in *Theological Studies,* September 1949) is Max Pribilla, S. J., who says that "the Church cannot demand freedom for herself in one state as a human right, and deny it in another state, according as Catholics are in a minority or a majority."

Another is Father Jacques Ledlercq of the University of Louisiana, who admits, at least indirectly, that there is an uncomfortable similarity between the traditional Roman Catholic procedure and that of the political totalitarians. He "has the impression" that the Church "will never bless a Catholic country which would apply in the service of the faith a policy parallel to that which the Soviets practice in favor of their conceptions." Our thanks for this up-to-date information is gladly given to the editors of the *Federal Council Bulletin.*

That Roman Catholic laymen are troubled is evidenced by articles which have recently been published in magazines. For example, in *Harper's Magazine* of November 1949, there appeared an article, "The Catholic Controversy," by George N. Shuster, president of Hunter College, a Catholic educator who is interested in truth, fair play and good will. In this article he cites the typical views held by Catholics and non-Catholics about each other.

The non-Catholic says:

The strength of the Catholic Church can inspire uneasiness and fear. On a trip up the Hudson, one passes rows of former estates now chock-full of priests, nuns, and brothers working diligently to make America Catholic. They take their orders from their own brand of Comintern—that is, the Vatican.

Were they to succeed, what would be the lot of dissenters? Does not the Church teach that once Catholics have gained control of the state they must abolish the civil rights of those outside the fold? Do they not do so wherever they can?[7]

Dr. Shuster says, "The Catholic counterattack is not without zest and flavor," and he states the views of some Catholics:

Protestantism is in a state of decomposition. It believes in nothing, not even the Divinity of Christ, and cannot agree to support any ethical principle. This sorry condition is the consequence of having been in error since the Reformation. . . .

Protestants are unimaginative, staid, stubborn, blue-nosed, and addicted to innocuous public prayers on insignificant occasions.[8]

He goes on to say:

When one bears in mind that the majority of Americans are to be found in neither camp, but that there is abroad in the land a notably wistful hope that religion might help us all to find a path across the landscape modern man is fated to inhabit, the spectacle of two great Confessions locked in mutually destructive battle is disheartening.[9]

---

[7] George N. Shuster, "The Catholic Controversy," *Harper's Magazine* (November 1949), p. 25.

[8] *Ibid.*, p. 26

[9] *Ibid.*, p. 26.

Dr. Shuster concludes his able article with this statement: "I have just one bit of advice to offer: it will not help to play ostrich one minute and firebrand the next."

Another article appeared in *Harper's Magazine* of May 1950, entitled "The Catholic Church in America," by another Catholic layman, D. W. Brogan. It is given over largely to the consideration of Paul Blanshard's book, *American Freedom and Catholic Power,* but the important thing about the article is a veiled plea for the open discussion of religious questions in America.

In spite of these questioning voices the stand of the Roman Catholic Church is firmly maintained. How did it arrive at these conclusions? By claiming of divine right of Apostolic succession, direct from St. Peter. It was early acclaimed, and came to be accepted by the Roman Catholics that the Roman pontiff was a lineal successor to the Apostle Peter, who founded the Church at Rome. The peculiar prestige which Jesus supposedly gave Peter is described in Matthew 16:17-19:

And Jesus answered and said unto him, Blessed art thou, Simon Bar-jona: for flesh and blood hath not revealed *it* unto thee, but my Father which is in heaven. And I say also unto thee, That thou art Peter, and upon this rock I will build my church; and the gates of hell shall not prevail against it. And I will give unto thee the keys of the kingdom of heaven: and whatsoever thou shalt bind on earth shall be bound in heaven: and whatsoever thou shalt loose on earth shall be loosed in heaven.

The Roman Catholic Church claimed this power was transferred to Peter's successors, the Roman pontiffs.

The divine right of kings is now an anachronism; so also should be the divine right of popes. The story is told of the late Dr. S. Parkes Cadman and Cardinal Gibbon, who, when crossing the Atlantic Ocean on their return from a summer spent in Europe, engaged in conversations. These two able religious leaders were sincere friends, and they talked at length every day of their journey about their common concern for the will of God to be known and practiced by men.

In the conversations Cardinal Gibbon naturally told of his visit to the Pope, which was the high point of his trip. Dr. Cadman was interested in the account, but finally in a courteous yet frank manner asked Cardinal Gibbon, "How do you account for his—the Pope's—infallibility?"

"I don't," Gibbon replied. "He called me 'Jibbon.'"

Of course it is a story but it has point to it. We Protestants believe that only God is infallible. And so do all thoughtful people who do not have their tongues in their cheeks.

The conclusion of the matter is that the totalitarian state claims the right to prescribe what its citizens read and think. It insists that every teacher, every professor, every editor, every writer and every commentator shall teach only what it approves. This also is the philosophy and practice of the totalitarian church. The Protestant Church does not and cannot tolerate this, for its members believe that coercing people to believe this or that which is prescribed and must be accepted with or without question is contrary to that freedom which God guarantees to every man.

In the countries of Europe you will find the deadening hand of political and religious oppression is laid heavily. This is not true, as yet, in America and we must not become lax and give up our great heritage of freedom. The separation of the State and the Church in America is our most effective bulwark against the usurpation of the rights of the individual by the State. The totalitarian state can never flourish in a nation where one is free to choose his own religion. Political and religious freedom are interrelated.

Once the freedom of the soul is lost, free speech, free conscience, free assembly and free press, et cetera, are lost. On the other hand, as long as the freedom of thought and decision is maintained, all other freedoms can be sustained and furthered.

As has been said before, with the world menaced by Communism and secularism, all the religious forces ought to be working together against our common foes. If this gulf between Catholics and Protestants widens much farther, it may result in making all of us, Catholics and Protestants, "second-class" (as the Catholics often term the Protestant religion) men in a society in which religion itself shall have been ruled irrelevant. God forbid!

It is the commonly accepted idea to think of a Protestant as one who is resisting something he does not like. Such a negative meaning would define a Protestant as one who is against. This is an unfortunate misnomer and not the truth. In fact, the negative meaning of this word *against* is at best only a secondary interpretation of the term *protestant*. The antagonistic word is *contestant,* not *protestant*. The Latin prefix *pro* means *for* while *con* means *against*. In Latin *testis* means *witness* or *to be a witness*. The first definition for the word *protest* is, according to Webster: "to assert, to aver, to affirm." To protest, therefore, means basically to testify or to witness.

Protestant is a noble, positive and constructive word. A Protestant is one who bears testimony to his own personal convictions. Protestantism is a witnessing religion. When a Protestant becomes only a contestant, he has fallen from his true role. To be *anti* alone is to be negative, and is not a worthy motivation for either thought or deed. Of course if it be a negative thing to remove that which is harmful, then there is value in being "against." It is often necessary to remove diseased tissue from the body as a preliminary to the regaining of health. But with the things of the Spirit, this is not the primary thing. Jesus said, "Ye shall be my witnesses." We Protestants are witnesses, witnesses for Christ and his redemptive power. We must personally and collectively show our faith. The emphasis must be affirmative rather than negative. The true Protestant is one who is ready to bear testimony on behalf of something real and vital. He is a witness of the truth of God as revealed in Jesus Christ. Silence in the face of wrong is the pathway to slavery, therefore the Protestant must consistently bear his witness.

These are some of the reasons why, one by one, we are compelled to proclaim, "I am a Protestant," and therefore are forced to decline the Pope's invitation.

2

THE PROTESTANT WITNESS

SOME Protestants hesitate to consider this subject of Protestant and Catholic differences for fear that they may be misunderstood. There are those who say, "This is not the thing to do. When we begin to point out differences between Protestantism and Roman Catholicism, we are apt to excite prejudice in the minds of people, and the world is already suffering from too much prejudice and bigotry." Yet why should we hesitate to consider any matter of religious faith? Indeed, we must be tactful in the sense of being thoughtful and considerate, lest we offend and do real harm by increasing already strained relationships, rather than help to lessen prejudice and improve relationships. But we must examine the facts. "The unexamined life is unlivable," said Plato.

The late Jan Christiaan Smuts has well stated the cause of our divisions: "The disease of the world is fragmentation; the cure of the world is holism, and that is God." He called his theory *holism* from the Greek word for *whole*. The main trend of evolutionary development, he contended, is the building of more complicated wholes. "Ours is a whole-making universe. We are interrelated."

Dr. Paul J. Tillich has expressed the same idea in somewhat different terms. He says, "The disease of the world is brokenness; the cure of the world is unity."

Dr. E. Stanley Jones tersely concludes, "It is time that the

32

Church and Christians cease being a part of the disease and become a part of the cure."

Nevertheless, this subject, "The Protestant Witness," must not be avoided. We Protestants have the right to consider it, and it is our duty to do so. Protestants must know why they are Protestants, why they become Protestants and what are the fundamental differences between the Protestant Church and the Church of Rome. The reasons are many and obvious. A number of our Protestant young people are marrying Roman Catholics and turning Catholic for them, saying, "After all, their Church demands it, and that is all there is to it." College students and young people in general often remark to a religious leader, "My Catholic roommate is very sure about his faith; he has ready answers as to what he believes, but I really don't know what I believe or why I believe what I do believe." Increasingly, Protestant young people are going to their religious leaders and asking, "What is it we Protestants believe?"

The thoughtful men and women who are living in our modern "satellite towns" in the outskirts of our cities wish to know, "Why is each of the major denominations interested in building a little church of its own persuasion in our community? Why don't they combine their efforts and help us to build one plant suitable for all Protestants and make it possible for us to secure an able minister and an adequate church staff?" When they find no satisfactory response, they ask, "What is the matter with the statesmanship of the Protestant Church?"

The Protestant Church must be awakened to the realization of its great genius: the ability to help people take charge of their own lives under God and live transformed and transforming lives; the possibilities of extending the ideals of democracy with its resultant dignity of personality throughout our land and in all the world and the latent strength in the denominations uniting to build more effectively what we Christians call the Kingdom of God on earth.

Protestants and Roman Catholics alike believe in God, in Jesus Christ as Lord and Saviour, in the good life, and in immortality. The Apostles' Creed belongs to all of us. Thoughtful Protestants believe that the forms these essential doctrines take must more closely conform to those which Jesus taught by word, deed and life. Their ideas came, in part, from the Reformation, which like all revolutions, was very complicated. The Reformation was a reaction against the misrepresentation of Christianity by the medieval Church. Martin Luther and his contemporaries in the Protestant Reformation first challenged the validity of the Church's grant of authority to the priests because so many of the latter were non-Christlike in exercising it. Furthermore, as they went back to the New Testament, they discovered that the spirit, attitudes and practices of many priests were in marked contrast to those principles enunciated by Jesus.

A brief interpretation of church history is needed for us to understand the Protestant Reformation. The Apostolic Church grew up in the latter part of the first century and was particularly strong in the second and third centuries. Persecution followed because the devotion of the members of the Apostolic Church to Christ, manifested in faith and practice, interfered with the pagan beliefs and corrupt practices of those in power.

In the fourth century the persecution of Christians ceased because Constantine, the Emperor, believed that the symbol of the Cross on his banner had brought him victory in battle. He accepted Christianity and decreed that it should be the official state religion. This resulted in large numbers of people, who like Constantine had little, if any, spiritual awareness of what it meant to be a Christian, becoming enrolled in the Church.

For the next six or seven hundred years, in spite of internal controversies and differences with the ruling kings, the Church was united. In 1054, differences between the Church in Western Europe and the Eastern Church resulted in a separation known as the "Great Schism." The Catholic Church became divided into the Roman Catholic and Eastern Orthodox Churches and remained so for five centuries. The Protestant Reformation divided again the Roman Catholic Church which had not been Catholic, that is, wholly one and universal, for five centuries.

By the thirteenth century the Papacy had reached the peak of its power and for approximately two centuries rivaled even the Roman Empire itself. Later, when the Empire was broken up into nations, the Papacy still maintained its place as the dominant spiritual authority in Western Europe.

The Reformation was focused on Martin Luther of Germany, who truly set the match to the fuse. The reasons which drove him to think and act as he did were many. Among these was his denial of the absolute claim of authority of the Pope and the church hierarchy. Also, he became alarmed at many of the corrupt practices which had gradually and devastatingly crept into the Church. He rejected, as foreign to the original teaching and spirit of Christianity, the holy water, the adoration of Mary, veneration of the saints, penance, i.e., the doctrine of good works, purgatory, and especially the sale of indulgences.

While the [Roman Catholic] church teaches that, in order to approach the confessional worthily, one must have contrition, or, in other words, the sincere sorrow that springs from hatred of sin for its own sake, many theologians maintain that, when this is lacking, attrition, or the sorrow that springs from fear of punishment, is sufficient. So penance has often been conceived by Roman Catholics in an external way, and ceremonial acts done at the direction of the priest have been re-

garded as relieving the sinner of the temporal punishment
which would otherwise be visited upon his sin. Through the
granting of indulgences (i.e., permission to substitute an easier
for a more severe penance), the merit stored up by Christ and
the saints becomes available for further remission of temporal
punishment, which may be used by the one to whom the indulgence is granted, either for his own benefit or for that of
suffering souls in purgatory.[1]

Luther uttered his protest against these grotesque and pagan
practices.

Tersely stated, the Reformation stressed this difference in
belief: The Protestants believe that one becomes a Christian,
not by the miraculous power of the sacraments, as the Catholics contend, but in the confession of faith that God's grace
and power as revealed through Jesus Christ is the essential
truth.

The Protestant Reformation was more than a reaction
against a misrepresentation of Christianity; it was a positive
and progressive movement. As Abdel Wentz, an able authority on Luther's life, points out:

Luther's movement was not a negative or reactionary movement. . . . It was not merely a sudden revolt against the immediate past, an impulsive throwing off of a mountain-load
of errors in the official ecclesiastical apparatus of salvation; on
the contrary, it was the logical outcome of the centuries, the
continuation of the deepest and most vital elements in the
Christian piety.[2]

The reformers maintained that entanglement of useless ritu-
alism and ecclesiasticism was a barrier to the Spirit of Christ

---

[1] William Adams Brown, *Beliefs That Matter* (New York, Charles Scribner's
Sons, 1928), pp. 262, 263. Reprinted by permission of the publishers.

[2] Abdel Ross Wentz, "Luther and His Tradition" in *Protestantism, a Symposium* (Nashville, Tenn., The Methodist Church, 1944), p. 42.

and prevented it from having power to grant "newness of life" to the earnest and honest believer.

The religious and economic conditions in Germany at the beginning of the sixteenth century were under severe criticism. Taxation and interference in churchly matters by the Pope greatly oppressed the people. There was widespread and just criticism of the clergy because of the unworthy examples of many of their number. The people in the cities were objecting to the clerical exemptions from taxation, the observance of so many holy days, and the Church's toleration of beggars. Monasteries were, in many places, badly in need of reform, and their large landholdings were viewed with disdain, both by the nobles who desired them and by the peasants who worked on the land. The peasants in general were in a state of economic unrest, not the least of their grievances being the fees exacted by the local clergy for penance. Many of the lay people and clergy were shocked by the immorality and greed of some of the clergy. In spite of the fact that in 384 a decree imposing celibacy upon all priests was issued by the Pope, there was gross laxity in its observance. In 1215 this decree was strengthened, and marriage of the priest was strictly forbidden. Although there were stricter regulations, the law of celibacy continued to be transgressed by many priests. Greed on their part was even more widespread and profaned the functions of their high calling.

The Renaissance was stirring the minds of intellectuals, and men like Peter Waldo, John Wycliffe and John Huss were awakening the common people to a new interpretation of religion as a vital force in the life of the individual. It was evident that the various shortcomings and sins that were prevalent in the church would meet opposition and, furthermore, a positive expression. This came through a priest, Martin Luther, who became a fearless yet constructive leader.

Martin Luther

Martin Luther was born on November 10, 1483, in Eisleben in Saxony. Both his father and mother were good people of simple background. His father was a miner, a man of vigor and self-reliance which enabled him to win something more than average success. He was sensible in his attitude toward life in general, and outwardly he seemed to have a complacent attitude toward many of the prevalent religious practices. His independence, however, was revealed in his reply to a visiting priest when he lay ill, who urged him to purchase his peace with God through gifts to the clergy. He replied: "I have many children. I will leave my property to them—they need it more." His piety had a practical turn which caused him to put the emphasis on everyday responsibilities, and it was his constant endeavor to meet his obligation to the members of his family which he considered his highest duty.

Luther's mother had a marked influence upon his life; she faced the world with a simple faith and was an optimist prepared for the worst. Her cheerfulness in spite of hardships was a trait her son found of invaluable aid to him in his future days and brought solace to him in many of "the dark hours of his soul."

His parents moved from Eisleben to Mansfeld soon after Martin's birth. There, his father was convinced that it was his duty to give his son an education that would fit him for a career in law. After attending school in Mansfeld, Magdeburg and Eisenach, Luther entered the University of Erfurt in 1501, where he was known as an earnest, music-loving and fun-loving student.

The sudden death of a friend and his own escape from death by lightning caused Luther to give up his study of law, and in July 1505, at the age of twenty-one, he entered the monastery of Augustinian hermits in Erfurt. The Augustinian monastery, most favorably noted for its learning and public service, was one of eight in Erfurt.

Luther's decision to enter the monastery came rather late in life as compared with the other young men of his time who planned to study for the priesthood. This fact had considerable influence on Luther and to a large extent affected the actions of the remainder of his life. Scholars are in general agreement that, because some of the most impressionable years of Luther's early life were spent in the stimulating atmosphere of a university rather than in a monastery, he was aware of the problems under normal conditions which are common to mankind. These factors were reflected in his later writings and influenced the polity and organization of the Protestant Church, of which he was the founder. His sympathetic understanding of the problems and the difficulties involved in living the good life grew out of his own varied experience and the struggle to gain mastery over life through self-imposed discipline.

In the monastery, Luther was zealous in his piety and devotion and faithful to a fault in all of his duties. "If ever a monk gained heaven by his monkery," he once wrote, "I must have done so. All the brethren who knew me will bear me witness. For I should have martyred myself, if I had kept it up longer, with watching, praying, reading and other labors."

He was ordained to the priesthood in 1507, taking the threefold vow of poverty, chastity and obedience, repeating the oath:

I, Brother Martin, make profession and promise obedience to Almighty God, to the Holy Virgin Mary, to the Holy Father Augustine, and to thee, the prior of this convent, who standest in the place of the General of the Order, to live until death in poverty and chastity, according to the rule of the said Father Augustine.

The ordination service made a deep impression on Luther, and the memory of the scene and the solemn vows taken were often in his thoughts and were frequently mentioned in his writings. It was with great difficulty and with much searching of soul that later he broke these vows.

The supreme question for Luther was: "What can I do to win the favor of God?" His ardent endeavor to find peace of mind ended in defeat. He could not rid himself of a tragic sense of sinfulness. His agony was so intense that those around him were greatly concerned about his troubled and confused mental attitude and health of mind. Johann von Staupitz, a highly respected priest, helped him to the understanding that true penitence began, not with the fear of an angry and punishing God, but through His forgiving love, based not on any work of merit on man's part but on absolute faith in God and His promise. This new and joyous relationship to God through Christ resulted in a new life of willing conformity to God's will. Augustine's idea, "Love God and do as you please," helped Luther as he came to the glorious realization that, if one pleases to love God, one will love to please Him.

This idea was a rediscovery and re-emphasis of a most important part of Paul's teaching. Yet it was more than Pauline. To Paul, the Christian is primarily a renewed moral being. To Luther, he is first of all a forgiven sinner, but Luther, like Paul, made salvation essentially a right personal relationship with God. The reconciling love of God was not dependent upon good works. The German mystics, especially John Tauler, the preacher who denounced both excessive ritual and good works, led Luther to the conclusion that salvation was not, as he had been taught as a priest, largely dependent on works but was wholly the gift of God. The lectures on Romans, which Luther gave in 1515-1516, did much to intensify these basic convictions. The idea of salvation through works now had been overthrown in Luther's thinking.

He did not readily attain complete peace of mind. He needed further conviction, and it came in large measure from the further study of Paul's writings. In the latter part of his lectures on Romans, the belief that the God-given nature of faith involves personal assurance became a real conviction. Thus after an intense personal struggle and long searching of the New Testament, the truth came to him that the pardon he sought was the free gift of God to be had by faith in Jesus Christ. He restated Paul's great doctrine, "The just shall live by faith."

The truth that faith in God, as He is made known in Jesus Christ, brings its reward of spiritual insight, grace and peace, is the dominant theme of the New Testament. Therefore, the New Testament teaching of "justification by faith"—a personal faith that one is justified, made right with God—was not only the key to Luther's new faith but the symbol of that of the reformed faith as well.

In the year 1517 opportunity presented itself for Luther to use this new conception of salvation. A Dominican prior, John Tetzel, "a preacher of great popular power," was sent by the Pope into a part of Germany to oversee the traffic of indulgences. The reason for this sale of indulgences was twofold: funds were needed by Pope Leo X for the enlarging of the Church of Saint Peter in Rome, and the Bishop and Elector of Mayence, Albert of Brandenburg, needed a large amount of money in order to pay back to John Fugger, the banker, money which he had borrowed to pay Rome for the privilege of assuming an archbishopric. In order to enable him to meet his obligation, the Pope permitted indulgences to be sold in that part of Germany which was under Albert's jurisdiction, half of the money to go to Albert and half to the Papacy.

Pope Leo X proclaimed a so-called "plenary indulgence," which offered the purchasers many benefits, such as remission of sins, freedom from penance, and even promised freedom from purgatory to the purchasers and their deceased friends and loved ones.

The doctrine of indulgences needs to be understood. It was based on the Catholic penitential system which held that the Papacy, since it had the keys to heaven and hell, had also the keys to the storehouse of merit. It was the Pope's privilege and power to grant remission of temporal penalties of sin, including penance in this life and the punishment in purgatory. Thus the Church not only claimed power to free the living from the future pains of purgatory but also to remove the dead from purgatory.

The term *indulgence* is defined by the official catechism of the Roman Catholic Church as "the remission of the temporal punishment which often remains due to sin after its guilt has been forgiven." This remission may be either total (plenary) or partial according to the terms of the indulgence. Such remission was popularly called a "pardon."

In the Early Church penance was regarded as an expression of repentance before sinners could be reconciled to God. The Roman Catholic Church, however, changed this concept of penance and substituted the idea that sins could only be atoned for by meritorious works. Although the Church had regular prescribed forms of penance, alternate forms were frequently allowed. The permission granting the substitution was called an "indulgence."

The granting of these permissions was often very much abused. For example, during the Crusades the Pope often told the soldiers of the Cross that their service would be accepted in full discharge of the penance otherwise required of them. Naturally, this form of indulgence encouraged enlistments in the service. After the Crusades had come to a close, the Papacy was not slow to realize that the granting of indulgences was a convenient method to employ when money was needed.

The whole indulgence traffic, particularly as it existed in the fifteenth and sixteenth centuries, was harmful in the extreme. There was the constant temptation, on the one hand, to employ it to raise funds for selfish ends, and, on the other hand, to substitute the mere payment of money for true penitence and amendment of life. Both temptations were frequently yielded to, and the result was wide-spread and growing demoralization.[3]

This is the conclusion reached by Dr. McGiffert in *Martin Luther, the Man and His Work.*

Luther, like many other good Catholics, priests and laymen, in the earlier days as well as his own, severely criticized the abuse of indulgences. When John Tetzel came to the neighborhood bordering on Luther's parish, Luther voiced his protest. Tetzel did not enter Luther's parish because the church could not offer the sale of indulgences without the consent of the civil authorities, a permission Frederick the Wise would not grant in his lands for churches elsewhere. Nevertheless, the powerful appeal of Tetzel tempted some of Luther's parish to cross the near-by border and purchase letters of indulgence which were being sold.

The following passage from one of Tetzel's sermons reveals the strong appeal to the fears of his hearers:

Do you hear your dead parents crying out "Have mercy upon us! We are in sore pain and you can set us free for a mere pittance. We have borne you, we have trained and educated you, we have left you all our property, and you are so

[3] Arthur Cushman McGiffert, *Martin Luther, the Man and His Work* (New York, The Century Company, 1910, 1911), p. 80. Reprinted by permission of the publishers.

hard-hearted and cruel, that you leave us to roast in the flames
when you could so easily release us."

The selling of indulgences and the growing abuses of the
practice were frowned on by many of the conscientious people
and led them to question the practice itself. They began asking
themselves and one another about the influence it would have
on their community, economically, morally and spiritually.

The members of Luther's parish who had purchased letters
of indulgence from Tetzel presented them to Luther at confession. He refused to accept them in place of repentance and
penance. They entered their complaints with Tetzel, and as
a result Luther was threatened with prosecution for heresy.

Quick as he [Luther] had hitherto been to denounce any evil
confronting him, now in the face of the worst and most crying abuse yet encountered, he took careful counsel with himself. . . . The present campaign, he saw clearly enough, was
far more demoralizing than anything he had preached against
in the castle church; but it was carried on under the auspices
of the primate of Germany and of the pope himself, and it
would not do to attack it recklessly and indiscriminately. He
must discover, if he could, the right and wrong of the whole
matter. . . . He had a conscience which made indifference impossible.[4]

Luther's conscience was enraged, so in accordance with a
custom of the times, on October 31, 1517, he nailed his Ninety-
five Theses concerning indulgences on the door of the Witten-
berg Church. The posting of these articles was not intended
as an offense, but he thereby published his views.

Attached to the theses was the following announcement:

In the desire, and with the purpose, of elucidating the truth, a
disputation will be held on the subjoined propositions at Wit-

---

[4] *Ibid.,* p. 87.

tenberg, under the presidency of the Reverend Father Martin
Luther, Augustinian monk, master of arts and of sacred theology, and ordinary lecturer upon the same in that place. He
therefore asks those who cannot be present and discuss the
subject orally to do so by letter in their absence.

In his theses Luther attacked both the theory and the practice of indulgences. He denounced them as contrary to the
gospel and the teaching of Jesus. He could see no reason for
indulgences except as a means for raising money. He condemned the right of papal authority over God and conscience.
He further condemned the use of indulgences, and especially
the sale of them, as detrimental to the individual, interfering
with his nurture and growth as a true believer and faithful
follower of the true gospel.

His indictments of indulgences were so complete that in
his eyes they were stripped of all religious value. Proof of
his severe indictment of indulgences is found in the thirty-
sixth and thirty-seventh theses, where he declared:

Every Christian who feels true compunction has of right
plenary remission of punishment and guilt without letters of
indulgence.

Every true Christian whether living or dead, has a share
in all the benefits of Christ and the church, given him, by
God, even without such letters.

Tetzel knew that, if these statements were believed, his sale
of indulgences was ruined forever. Therefore, he attempted
to justify his position as a dealer in the traffic of indulgences,
and the sale of indulgences on the order of the Pope as well,
by sending out statements to counteract the condemnation in
Luther's theses. His main statement dealt with the infallibility
of the Pope, a doctrine held by the Church since the latter
part of the Middle Ages. He contended that Christians should
accept the following:

The authority of the pope is superior to that of the universal church and council, and his statutes must be humbly obeyed.

The pope cannot err in those things which are of faith and necessary to salvation.

They who speak slighteningly of the honor and authority of the pope are guilty of blasphemy.

Later on Pope Leo attempted to silence Luther by issuing a papal bull, or edict. Luther's reaction is expressed in the following words:

I hoped the pope would protect me, for I had so fortified my theses with proofs from the Bible and papal decretals that I was sure he would condemn Tetzel and bless me. But when I expected a benediction from Rome, there came thunder and lightning instead, and I was treated like the sheep who had roiled the wolf's water. Tetzel went scot-free, and I must submit to be devoured.

The conflict between the suporters of Pope Leo and Luther and his adherents continued with increasing intensity. In August 1520 Luther, becoming more and more convinced that he could not avoid an open break with the Roman Catholic Church, published a notable document entitled *Address to the German Nobility*. In his dedication to a fellow priest, Amsdorf, he wrote:

The time for silence is past and the time to speak is come, as the preacher Solomon says. In conformity with our resolve I have put together a few points concerning the reformation of the Christian estate in order to lay them before the Christian nobility of Germany in case it may please God to help His church by means of the laity, since the clergy whom this task rather befitted have grown quite careless. I send it all to your worship to judge, and to amend where needed. I am well aware that I shall not escape the reproach of taking too much upon me presuming, despised and insignificant man as I am, to address such high estates on such weighty subjects, as if there were no one in the world but Dr. Luther to have a care for Christianity and to give advice to such wise people. I offer no excuse. Let who will blame me. Perhaps I owe God and the world another folly. This debt I have now resolved honestly to discharge, if I can, and to be court fool for once. If I fail, I have at least one advantage, that no one need buy me a cap or shave my poll. But it remains to be seen which shall hang the bells on the other. I must fulfil the proverb "When anything is to be done in the world a monk must be in it were it only as a painted figure."

I beg you to excuse me to the moderately wise for I know not how to deserve the favor and grace of the overwise. Often I have sought it with much labor, but henceforth will neither have nor care for it. God help us to seek not our glory but His alone.

Luther already had the support of friends like Frederick the Wise, the prince of Saxony, and Ludwig of Palatinate. This *Address to the German Nobility* added many new friends to his cause, for many German people were in accord with him in his political as well as ecclesiastical declaration of independence from the Roman Empire and the Roman Church.

The Pope acted promptly and excommunicated Luther, who in turn promptly burned the decree of excommunication. The Pope sought to have him condemned by the Holy Roman Empire. A congress of the Empire, called a diet, was meeting in the German city of Worms, and Luther was summoned to appear before it for trial. His prince, Frederick the Wise, insisted that he be fairly heard and secured a promise that he would be returned home safely.

In April 1521, Luther stood before the princes of Germany and the Emperor Charles, a devout adherent to the Catholic faith. In his examination Luther was shown a number of books and asked if they were his. If so, he was to take back everything in them. He listened as the list was read and said that they were his. However, he asked time to think over the request to reject what was in them. This request for additional time was reluctantly granted, his answer to be forthcoming the following day. Many have conjectured that Luther had entered the place of trial not quite aware of what he was to face, and that he had asked for time that he might meditate upon his answer in order to make it as concise and final as he desired it to be.

When Luther appeared for examination the next day, he was again asked, "Do you defend all, or do you care to reject a part?" He spoke at length defending the contents of his writings. Eck, who had asked him the question interrupted, saying "I ask you, Martin—do you or do you not repudiate your books and the errors which they contain?" Luther replied:

Since then Your Majesty and lordships desire a simple reply, I will answer without horns and without teeth. Unless I am convicted by Scripture and plain reason—I do not accept the authority of popes and councils, for they have contradicted each other—my conscience is captive to the Word of God. I cannot and I will not recant anything, for to go against conscience is neither right nor safe. God help me. Amen.[5]

Some versions have the popularly quoted words: "Here I stand. I cannot do otherwise." The words, however, are not found in Luther's account of his speech but may have been added later.

The Emperor declared that he was sorry that he had delayed so long in acting against Luther for his false teaching. He condemned his obstinate defense of his theses and writings. As Frederick the Wise had demanded, he allowed him to return home under safe conduct but insisted that he should not

---

[5] Roland H. Bainton, *Here I Stand* (New York and Nashville, Abingdon-Cokesbury Press, 1950), p. 185. Reprinted by permission of the publishers.

do any preaching or make any tumult. He further condemned him as a notorious heretic and asked his electors to stand with him as they had promised. The electors seemingly were in accord with the will of the emperor, but two of them, Frederick of Saxony and Ludwig of Palatinate, proved themselves friends of Luther.

While in hiding, where he had been hurried by friends, Luther spent the time to good advantage. He wrote many letters and articles. Perhaps the most important thing that he did was to translate the Bible into German, first the New Testament and later the Old Testament. His translation of the Bible was just what was needed by the German people. "I endeavored," said he, "to make Moses so German that no one would suspect he was ever a Jew." The majesty of diction, elegance of style and religious conviction of Luther's translation made the Bible not only a great educational tool but the beloved Book of Life for those who read it.

Luther exemplified great courage in defending his beliefs and defying the Roman Church. Every resource of the Church and empire were used in the attempt to silence him. However, he influenced Frederick of Saxony deeply, and soon a number of other German princes joined the reform movement, thereby declaring their independence of Rome. Luther had become the prophet of a new faith and had the backing of men of influence.

Among the articles written by Luther was one entitled *The Babylonian Captivity of the Church,* in which he condemned the tradition in regard to sacraments which hung as a stone around the neck of Christianity, and urged reforms in the matter. This idea of freedom or independence, which was at the very center of Luther's innermost thoughts, appeared often; and later in a tract entitled *The Freedom of a Christian Man,* he wrote in paradoxical statements: "A Christian man is a most free lord of all things and subject to no one; a Christian man is a most dutiful servant of all things and subject to every one." True it is that the free man is the most bound. Also true it is that the Christian is bound in his freedom—bound to Christ, his Master.

The result of this freedom was evident at the First Diet of Speyer, held in the year 1526. At this meeting the decision was made that each German prince should determine the religion of his own state. This was the beginning of the official acceptance of Lutheranism. In 1529, however, another, the Second Diet of Speyer, was held as the Pope and the Emperor sought to bring pressure to bear on those who were seeking to promote the Reformation movement. They were not willing to accept the decision made at the First Diet of Speyer. This gathering, "packed," that is, dominated by princes who were loyal to Rome and the Emperor, rescinded the right of a prince, principality or city to have self-determination in religious matters. Five princes, nevertheless, together with representatives of fourteen cities, protested this revocation as unfair and upheld the right of the minority to self-determination. The declaration of the evangelical estates was that "in things which concern the honor of God and the salvation of their souls, each one must stand before God and be responsible to Him." The proponents were called "Protestants," and this name thereafter was applied to the reformers. Thus the original meaning of the word *Protestant,* as we have noted, was a positive witness of those who insisted on the right of religious liberty. The word *Protestant* did not signify an objector, but rather one who made an avowal, an affirmation of belief that man must act according to his conscience under God, for "God is the Lord of the conscience."

Martin Luther is one of the few men of whom it may be said that the history of the world was profoundly altered by his work. He moved men by the power of his religious experience. He enabled them to find unshakable trust in God, and a direct personal relationship to Him, which brought a confident salvation that left no room for the elaborate hierarchal and sacramental structure of the Roman Catholic Church. He spoke to his countrymen as a man who was profoundly one of them in aspirations and sympathies. So largely was he one of his race in virtues and limitations that he is often understood with difficulty by those not of German extraction.

Roland H. Bainton, Professor of Ecclesiastical History at Yale Divinity School and one of the country's leading specialists in Reformation history, has given us a notable and most vivid pen picture of Luther:

He was the father of a household, the molder of the German people, a new David playing on his harp, an emancipator of certain fetters of the spirit, the divider of the Church, and at the same time the renewer of Christendom. All this he was, and more; but pre-eminently for his own time as well as for ourselves he was a man athirst for God.[6]

It is a somewhat difficult task to sum up the work of any great historical figure such as Martin Luther, but his influence as a leader of the Reformation is of primary importance in the history of Protestantism and affects the Protestant movement even to this day. Luther was a product of the age in which he lived. The modern world owes him a great debt, aye, a debt eternal, because he broke the power of the Roman Catholic Church and set men free to find God and His purpose for their lives. The authority of the Catholic Church had to be challenged and limited before men could have this freedom to seek and find God, each according to his own conscience.

Lutheranism took possession of Scandinavia and has an extensive following in the United States, and apart from that

---

[6] From the jacket of *Here I Stand*.

his movement gave the impetus which sometimes launched and sometimes helped to establish the other varieties of Protestantism. They all stem in some measure from him. And what he did for his own people to a degree, he did also for others. His translation, for example, affected the English version. Tyndale's preface is taken from Luther. His liturgical reforms likewise had an influence on the *Book of Common Prayer*. And even the Catholic Church owes much to him. Often it is said that had Luther never appeared, an Erasmian reform would have triumphed, or at any rate a reform after the Spanish model. All of this is of course conjectural, but it is obvious that the Catholic Church received a tremendous shock from the Lutheran Reformation and a terrific urge to reform after its own pattern.[7]

In the midst of the storm and protests following the posting of his theses, Luther wrote to a former teacher at Erfurt, "I will do whatever the Lord gives me to do, and, God willing, never will I be afraid, or venture beyond what He commands." In that spirit he fought all his life to maintain the things that would advance this idea.

In his book, *Martin Luther, the Man and His Work,* Dr. McGiffert concludes:

He was built on no ordinary scale, this redoubtable German. He was of titanic stature, and our common standards fail adequately to measure him. But his life lies open to all the world, as do few other lives in history. To know it as we may is well worth an effort.[8]

In order that we may have an even broader knowledge of the background of Protestantism, it is well for us to recall the witness of some of the other early reformers who pioneered for the Protestant faith. In the next chapter we shall consider

7 Bainton, *Here I Stand,* p. 385.
8 McGiffert, *Martin Luther, the Man and His Work,* p. 388.

this witness. There we shall deal primarily with those who lived in the sixteenth century. Also, mention will be made of some noteworthy persons of a later period who belonged to the continuing reformation and bore their witness to the spirit and purpose of Christ. These could say in truth with St. Paul, "For me to live is Christ."

3

THE WITNESS OF THE OTHER REFORMERS

GREAT movements are largely the result of daring souls who help ideas become realities. With Victor Hugo they contend there is "nothing in the world so powerful as an idea whose time has come." The greatest battle is that being fought in the minds of men. So it was with the leaders of the Reformation; they had ideas whose time had come, and they helped determine the time.

The Protestant revolt against papal authority does not represent a purely religious movement. Rather was religion one of the most potent factors in an upheaval which was grounded in every aspect of the national and social life of those countries which came to adopt Protestantism. An understanding of the religious issue will be gained only from a survey of those other forces which contributed to the Protestant revolt.[1]

Among the contributing forces was the cultural movement known as the Renaissance, which was both ally and enemy to the religious reform movement. It was an ally in that it awakened an appreciation for the past and stimulated a desire to go back to the sources. It was an enemy to the religious reform movement because it made a cult of art and emphasized

---

[1] Cyril Charles Richardson, *The Church Through the Centuries* (New York, Charles Scribner's Sons, 1938), p. 132. Reprinted by permission of the publishers.

the worldliness and paganism of the Greco-Roman civilization. The Reformation owes a great debt to the Renaissance because it was an awakening to the values of antiquity as it sought to confirm truth through a turning to and searching of the sources. The sensitive priests and scholars of that day began to read again the New Testament and found there dominant religious convictions and a discipline for moral conduct.

This search produced great educational centers such as Deventer, Erfurt and Heidelberg and later Oxford. At these centers of learning the search for truth was carried on with particular emphasis given to the study of the New Testament, resulting in a devotion to the life and teaching of Christ. At Deventer, for example, Erasmus developed a passionate love for the New Testament. John Wimpfeling, one of the great teachers of his age and all time, who taught at Basel, wrote, "The better education of the young is the foundation of all true reform, ecclesiastical, national, and domestic. . . . Let study be for the quickening of the independent thought."

The Renaissance grew out of these educational centers, "the cathedral schools" of the Middle Ages. There grew up as a result a philosophic system known as Nominalism. The major ideas of this system were the belief that God speaks directly to each individual, that the true believers were joined together by faith and that the human will enabled man to change his nature for the better. These ideas were the bases of the theory and practice of the later Reformers.

It should be noted that the Reformation began within the Roman Catholic Church. The Protestant Reformation had put forth some sturdy roots before Luther, and was influenced by many movements and men.

A movement known as the Cathari had spread by the year 1200 throughout large parts of Italy, Spain and France. The adherents of this movement criticized with telling effect the

wealth of the Roman Catholic Church and challenged its power
and authority. They looked on the Bible as their authority.
They sought to purify the established sacraments by putting
emphasis on the Lord's Supper and baptism. Their followers
were recruited from the ranks of the poor and they opposed
the clergy and elevated the laity.

In 1176 Peter Waldo, a rich merchant of Lyons, France,
sold his goods because he took to heart the words of Jesus:
"Go, sell that which thou hast, and give to the poor, and thou
shalt have treasure in heaven: and come, follow me." He did
that, and went about among the common people reciting passages from the Bible, using a French translation of the New
Testament. He was joined by many others and they were
called "the poor men of Lyons." The Pope refused to grant
them permission to preach, but Waldo and his followers continued to do so, and they increased in numbers and grew in
power.

They rejected the doctrine of purgatory and prayers for the
dead, as they could not find any authority for these ideas in
the Bible. They were excommunicated by the Pope in 1184.

The Roman and French legions marched against these
brave souls for several years, until the Cathari movement was
completely crushed. The followers of Waldo, called the Wal-
denses, sought refuge in the valleys of the Alps and survived.
From that day, even to this day, they have been a potent force
in the religious life of the free church.

Ficino Marsilius of Padua was among those daring souls,
whose work was done in the fourteenth century. He bravely
advocated democratic practices for both Church and State, declaring that the source of the law is "the whole body of citizens
or the weightier part of them." Marsilius, in his *Defensor
Pacis,* proposed that the Church be governed by a general
council of representatives of all parts of the Church, "pious
men, priests and laymen." He ridiculed the idea of the papal

succession from St. Peter as the "saints legend," and contended that there was a parity of the priests. Marsilius and his followers were obliged to flee for their lives and were excommunicated by the Pope.

During the later part of the fourteenth century and throughout the fifteenth century the Roman Catholic Church reached an all-time low as far as corruption was concerned. This corruption invaded every form of life, financial, moral and spiritual, but "night brings out the stars." In every country there appeared a shining star of the pre-Reformation period. Gerhard Groot in Holland, John Wycliffe in England, Savonarola in Italy and John Huss in Bohemia raised their voices like trumpets demanding that the Church should be purified, that a new sense of ethical righteousness be instituted in the whole management and life of the ecclesiastical system of that day. Men like Groot set themselves to the task of promoting practical personal piety and social service. These and all of the other great teachers studied the classical languages with a new interest and were awakened to a new sense of the worth of the individual and a love for all mankind, even "the least, the last and the lost."

"Teachers of the Brethren" in Holland, as well as other schools began to print series of textbooks. These had great effect on the inquiring minds of young men throughout all Western Europe. For example, Ignatius Loyola, who read these books was started on his great career of reform. Luther and Calvin were indebted to these schools and to these books for inspiration and stimulation.

In England, John Wycliffe's moral earnestness and intellectual ability won for him the title "The Morning Star of the Reformation," although that term could be readily challenged. John Huss, the Bohemian reformer and martyr, was a disciple of Wycliffe. Huss was a man of action who by his beliefs and works attracted the attention of all Western Europe. His earnest and independent study of the Scriptures influenced him to hold views that the Scripture is the only law of the Church, that the Papacy must be subject to the law of the Scriptures, and that the Church itself is the only body of believers. These views eventually led to his being burned for heresy in 1415. Others like Francis of Assisi and Waldo held to the same views, but Huss had the honor of having been the chief intermediary in handing on, from Wycliffe to Luther, the torch which kindled the Reformation.

Erasmus, the greatest humanist of his day, was not simply a humanist, but also a religious man with deep concern for the knowledge of spiritual truths to correct the evil conditions of his day. He undertook to show that true piety consists in following Christ, obeying his precepts: "Think not that Christ is an empty voice. On the contrary count him nothing else than charity, simplicity, patience, purity, in short whatever he himself taught." Two special weapons, Erasmus said, a man needs in the conflict with sin: prayer and knowledge. In general, it could be said that Erasmus largely based his interpretation of Christianity on Jesus, while Luther based his on Paul.

Erasmus was troubled by the prevailing religious conditions of his day, and was profoundly convinced of the need of a reformation. But he was not a revolutionist and wanted only such a reformation as could be brought about within the existing establishment by the peaceful process of education. He was a loyal Catholic to the end of his life—to break with the Catholic Church was the last thing he wished—but he did much to determine the mold and the mood that led to the break with the Roman Catholic Church, and the establishment of the Protestant Church.

Associated with Erasmus and known as the Oxford Reformers were two men whom he influenced greatly, namely John Colet and Thomas More. These men exercised great influence on the work of religious reform in England.

We could well consider Reformers like Melanchthon, who was acclaimed "the first theologian of the Reformation." In his book, *The Main Points,* he set forth in simple language the central teaching of the Scriptures concerning man, the Church and man's relationship to God.

Some students of the Reformation would select as very important the priest who came to Zurich, Switzerland, at the beginning of the year 1519 to be the "people's priest," the scholar and distinguished humanist, Ulrich Zwingli. He had studied at the University of Basel, and had there acquired Protestant principles from Thomas Wyttenbach ten years before Luther posted his Ninety-five Theses; but Zwingli continued loyal to the Church and worked for the papal interests. In the early years of his priesthood he received from the Pope a small pension "for the purchase of books." Later on, while visiting Italy, however, as chaplain to Swiss mercenaries, Zwingli became doubtful of papal aims and set himself to stamp out the mercenary activities of the Church in Switzerland.

At Zurich, Zwingli became famous as a "preacher for the times," who denounced luxury and vice and the military spirit, and who went straight to the Scriptures for his doctrines. In 1522 Zwingli published in German sixty-seven articles, very much like the theses of Luther, and a debate took place in the City Hall. At its close, the government approved the articles and decreed that priests throughout the country should preach nothing but what can be proved by the Holy Gospel and the pure Holy Scriptures. It was the beginning of the Reformation in Zurich.

All these Reformers mentioned had a part in the Reformation, yet the three names which are generally and popularly credited with belonging to "the great triumvirate" are Martin Luther, John Calvin and John Knox.

Great men need not that we praise them; the need is ours that we know them. They are our common heritage. Whether

we be of their faith or of another, whether our fathers fought
with them or with their enemies, whether we stand where they
stood or have traveled far on ways they dreamed not of, we
are the richer that they lived.[1]

This is the able and intriguing beginning of the monumental
book on *Martin Luther, the Man and His Work,* by Arthur
Cushman McGiffert, the distinguished teacher of Church History.

We have given consideration to Martin Luther in Chapter
II. Let us now evaluate the life and teaching of John Calvin.

John Calvin

In the year 1509 there was born at Noyon, Picardy, one
who gave to the Reformation intellectual stature. This man,
John Calvin, was one of the most influential and vigorous figures of a late phase of the Reformation. As Dr. Wilhelm
Pauck has truly said, "Calvin belongs to the second generation of reformers." When Calvin was born, Luther and Zwingli were in their middle twenties and the Reformation had
been inaugurated in Germany and in parts of Switzerland.

Calvin was influenced by his early environment which did
much to condition his thought life. France, at the end of the
fifteenth century and beginning of the sixteenth was conceded
to be one of the most advanced countries in all Europe in governmental organization and education. Francis I, ruler of that
time, greatly helped Calvin in his formative years. In addition
to Francis' personal charm, and in spite of his worldly ambition and lack of personal morality, he had an interest in and
sympathy with learning. He attracted to his court many people versed in arts and letters, and aided many a promising
young man in completing his education. Francis was the bene-
factor of the University of Paris, which had top rating among

---

[2] McGiffert, *Martin Luther, the Man and His Work,* p. 3.

other universities of Europe because of its noted teachers and high academic standing. Institutions of learning are but the lengthening shadows of their great teachers. The University of Paris numbered among its teachers of fame Aquinas and Duns Scotus. Its theological school, known as the Sorbonne, was founded in 1253 by Robert de Sorbon. This institution had the intellectual as well as the financial support of Francis I.

The influence of the Renaissance led men to investigate anew the original sources of religious truth. Among the leaders of this new awakening, one who deserves special mention was the great teacher Lefèvre of Etaples. He, more than any other man, prepared the way for Calvin's notable theological contributions.

John Calvin had a thorough education in French law and the classics. He was graduated in law, but shortly after his father's death in 1531, he gave up law and took up the study of the classics, specializing in Greek and Hebrew.

Calvin was about twenty years of age when he came directly under the influence of the Reformation. It is exceedingly difficult to make out clearly the process of his conversion from being a student supported from the Roman Catholic Church funds to that of being a follower and then a leader of Protestantism. The important factors that led him to take this step were his belief that the Scriptures alone were the voice of God and that God speaks through the recorded words of the Scriptures.

Four years later Calvin wrote an address for the University of Paris which contained his many reformed ideas and convictions, many of which were at variance with the established Church. An investigation followed and he was forced to flee for his life. He took refuge in Switzerland.

In the year 1536 he published the first edition of his great work. The *Institutes* were elaborated in the five editions from six to eighty chapters during Calvin's lifetime, although the basic thoughts remained in substance the same as those written when he was only twenty-six years of age.

These *Institutes* gave the Reformation a logical exposition of its doctrines. Writing in 1541, Calvin said of his treatise:

Although the Holy Scriptures contain a perfect doctrine, to which nothing can be added . . . still every person, not intimately acquainted with them, stands in need of some guidance and direction as to what he ought to look for in them. . . . This cannot be better done in writing than by treating in succession of the principal matters which are comprised in Christian Philosophy. For he who understands these will be prepared to make more progress in the school of God in one day than any other person in three months. . . . With this view I have composed the present book.

The purpose of the *Institutes* was to interpret and explain the Scriptures; above everything else Calvin made central in all of his thinking the sovereignty of God. God's will is unconditioned. In his theology the Bible was to him the sole authority of faith and morals.

The greater part of Calvin's lifework was carried on in Geneva. There he formed a Church-State relation, a representative form of government, based upon the New Testament, under the direction of representatives of the people called Elders. The system combined freedom with authority. Much of our civil liberty and representative democracy were due to the work of Calvin. In general, our representative democracy has two sources; first, the Greek with its emphasis on natural rights of men; second, the religious concept of the equality of men before God. This latter came in large measure from Calvinism. The Calvinists believed that it was a Christian duty to resist tyranny. This was based on the premise that each man has a personal relationship to God, and therefore is a creature of worth and dignity in the sight of God.

Another great contribution Calvinism made was in the realm of morality. Man was not only to acknowledge God as his sovereign power but he was to live the life God would have him live according to the definite divine plan for each life. Personal qualities of honesty, chastity, industry and integrity were obligatory for all Christians. Morality was recognized as something which was required both by the individual and society.

Calvin's theology was God-centered. In a spirit of humble obedience he ever sought to do God's will. He put God first, emphasizing His glory and sovereignty. The sinfulness of men and the saving work of Christ as revealed in the Bible were basic in his thought. In Calvin's exposition the theology of the Reformation age rose to a clearness and dignity of statement and a logical precision of definition that have never been surpassed. Calvin's system has stood the test of time better than most expositions of religious truths. The larger part of the Protestant faith, even in the churches which most honor his memory, has turned far aside from the literal application of his great truths. These cardinal truths are increasingly being recognized by thoughtful men as essential to a well-rounded Christian faith. While Calvin's system as a whole no longer has the allegiance it once commanded, it still exerts a profound influence on Christian thought and action and is the deadly foe of ignorance, superstition and magic.

The declaration of the Genevan Little Council accurately describes the prime motive of Calvin, this man of the sixteenth century, who possessed a Pauline intellect and a crusader's zeal. It said: "God gave him character of great majesty."

John Knox

Chief among those who went to Geneva and sat at the feet of Calvin was John Knox. He was a Scotsman, a rugged individualist who lived in a rugged time and country. The time and country in which he lived helped to shape this significant Reformation leader.

The Church historian, Williston Walker, has written, in his *Great Men of the Christian Church,* an able thumbnail sketch of Scotland before the Reformation:

His is not only the greatest figure in Scottish history, but the history of the Reformation in Scotland is largely the story of Knox's life.

Scotland before the Reformation was an undeveloped land. Its business and its culture were alike backward, it was torn by internal controversies in which the nobles and the great churchmen bore full share. Its monarchy was weak. Its church, though wealthy enough to possess half the land of the kingdom, was notoriously corrupt. In its political relations, Scotland was harassed by well-grounded fears of English aggression, which inclined the little kingdom to look for aid to France. The Reformation movement was far advanced on the Continent before it was felt in Scotland. The first Scottish Protestant martyr, Patrick Hamilton, was burned under Archbishop James Beaton at St. Andrews in 1528, and this policy of repression was even more severely carried out under James Beaton's nephew and successor, Cardinal David Beaton; but Protestantism grew very slowly till it found a leader in Knox.[3]

We do not know exactly when Knox was born, but it was about the year 1505. His parents enabled him to secure a good education. In the university he had as a teacher John Major, who was a devout Roman Catholic and yet was critical of the Papacy. He contended that the monks should be more carefully selected and fewer in number, and that civil authority was derived from the people.

Knox entered the priesthood in the year 1540, but in three

---

[3] Williston Walker, *Great Men of the Christian Church* (Chicago, University of Chicago Press, 1908), pp. 255, 256. Reprinted by permission of the publishers.

short years he was converted to Protestantism, partly as a result of the influence of Thomas Williams and George Wishart. His activities as a disciple of these two men made it impossible for him to remain in Scotland, so he assumed a pastorate at Berwick, England, and later in Newcastle. On his return to Scotland he and other Protestants were captured by the French in the battle for the Castle of Saint Andrews, and John Knox was made a galley slave on a French war vessel. After nineteen months of brutal slaving he was released in an exchange of prisoners and went to Europe, finally making his way to Geneva, attracted by Calvin's religious teaching. After some years he returned to England, and in the year 1555 he again went back to Scotland. The opposition there was so great that he finally returned to Geneva, where for four years he worked and studied under Calvin. He then went again to Scotland. The time was opportune there for Protestantism because Elizabeth, Queen of England, had given recognition to the growing movement.

With fearless and able leadership, John Knox championed the cause of Protestantism and that of the people against their ruler, Mary Queen of Scots, a Roman Catholic. They rallied to him and soon the Roman Catholic system was overridden and a Presbyterian system of government was introduced. In August 1560 the Presbyterian system (i.e., representative) of church government was adopted by the Scottish Parliament, thus giving a Presbyterian form to the national church of Scotland.

The Westminster Confession, as drafted by Knox and five associates, was adopted by the General Assembly of Scotland in 1647. This Confession was approved by the General Synod of the Presbyterian Church in America in 1729. The Westminster Confession, therefore, grew out of the work of John Knox, and Knox in turn owed much to John Calvin for his ideas both of doctrine and organization.

Among the distinctive ideas which John Knox instituted in

the Church of Scotland was the recognition of the parity, in the sense of equality, of all ministers. He showed remarkable executive ability in dividing Scotland into ten districts and placing superintendents over the districts. He enriched the Church by compiling a directory of worship. In this, the sermon was central.

An exciting and distinctive chapter in Scottish history is that of John Knox in his contest with Mary Queen of Scots. Mary stood for the right of the rulers to determine the prevailing religion while Knox stood for the right of the individual to choose his religion.

"What are you in this commonwealth?" Mary scornfully asked Knox in 1563.

"A subject born with the same," he replied, "and though neither earl, lord nor baron, God hath made me a profitable member."

The contest might have been more even, had it not been for Mary's misdeeds, her misfortunes and her sins.

Knox died in 1572. He had been a vigorous and fearless champion of the Christian cause until his death. Scotland is indebted to this great patriot, more than to anyone else, for her political and religious freedom. Here was a man who transferred religious power from the Pope to the people.

At the funeral in St. Giles Churchyard the new Regent Moray, under the guns of the imposing castle, made a fitting characterization in the often-quoted words: "Here lieth a man who in his life never feared the face of man." Knox himself a short time before had put in writing a larger claim for the historic future: "What I have been to my country, though this unthankful age will not know, yet the ages to come will be compelled to bear witness to the truth."

The influence of his life, like the soul of John Brown, goes marching on, and wherever men desire to be freed, the effect of Knox's teaching is felt. Some who live in these enslaving days claim relationship with him as a Scotsman, and an increasing number properly claim kinship with him in things of the spirit and hold it to be the saving fact in both political and religious realms that, as the late Dr. Nicholas Murray Butler, who for so many years was the President of Columbia University, said, "a free man is the hope of the world." That is true, but it is not all of the truth. The truth is this, a free man, socially minded and spiritually motivated, is the hope of the world.

Other Members of the Continuous Reformation

Thumbnail sketches of other men who belong to the continuing Reformation from the beginning should be considered here. As Hegel noted, we are lured by the ideal, and we organize to further the ideal, and then the organization stifles the ideal until it is impotent. So it was that the fresh creative epoch of the Reformation was followed by a new formalism. The lesser men who succeeded the great Reformers looked on the Reformation as essentially complete, so they settled back in self-sufficiency and complacency and the Protestant Church tended to become static and sterile.

Augustine is one of the best-known thinkers and shapers of early Christian thought. As a thinker he is ranked next to St. Paul; nevertheless, what he taught is little known to the average man.

Two of his sayings which have been widely quoted by ministers and laymen should be understood: "Love God and do as you please," and "Thou hast made us for Thyself, O God, and our hearts are restless until they find rest in Thee." Let us consider this second saying, for here the most vital truth in the world is compressed into one sentence. In it are portrayed the struggle of the seeking soul and the finding of the durable satisfactions which alone are realized in God and His purpose for our lives. In God is our rest, i.e., restoration, purpose and peace.

It would be well for religious people everywhere, particularly Christians, to read and reread "that masterpiece of psychology and religion"—*The Confessions of St. Augustine.* In this book and in his *City of God,* we see one of the first-rate minds of the whole Christian era come to grips with life and arrive at the conclusion that only God is great enough and good enough to satisfy the hunger of the human soul. Only when we love God with all our heart and soul and mind do we have all. Nothing else is satisfying or sufficient. "Not that we are sufficient of ourselves to think any thing as of ourselves; but our sufficiency *is* of God" (Second Corinthians 3:5). Truly the meaning of life is found in Augustine's profound statement, "Thou hast made us for Thyself, O God, and our hearts are restless until they find rest in Thee."

One of the outstanding examples of English religious thought was expressed by Richard Hooker, who died in 1600. His *Laws of Ecclesiastical Polity* was splendidly written, with superb literary style, logic and judgment. In this classic, concerning the Church and its theory of Church and State he set a pattern of thought, much of which has been followed in the Protestant English-speaking world.

Mention should be made of a greatly overlooked church leader. His name was Nikolaus Ludwig von Zinzendorf. He was the organizer and guiding spirit of the Herrnhut community in Saxony, which was formed in 1727. Ten years later he received his ordination as bishop in the reorganized Moravian church, or "United Brethren" as the body preferred to call itself. Zinzendorf was an organizer of marvelous talent. He devoted himself unreservedly to the service of his Master.

He voiced his piety in hymns, some of which, like "Jesus Still Lead On, Till Our Rest Be Won," have been loved by Christians everywhere. Few men have shown such personal devotion to Christ. He declared again and again, "I have only one passion. It is Christ, none but he."

Many men helped to redeem the Church from the dry-as-dust forms into which it had settled. At the beginning of the eighteenth century (1703), when England was in an age of "infidelity endemic" and corruption in the air (as Thackeray phrased it) and the state of the Church was at a very low point, John Wesley was born, and he lived almost to the century's end, dying in 1791. The outstanding feature of the age was its moral insensibility and irreligion. Few men have ever made so great a change in the moral and spiritual life of their day as Wesley.

Woodrow Wilson well said:

The Church was dead and Wesley awakened it; the poor were neglected and Wesley sought them out; the gospel was shrunken into formulas and Wesley flung it fresh upon the air once more in the speech of common men; the air was stagnant and fetid; he cleared and purified it by speaking always and everywhere the word of God; and men's spirits responded, leaped at the message and were made wholesome as they comprehended.

Wesley helped to free men from moral and spiritual insensibility in a darkened age. The English Reformation was in many ways unique, as it did not represent so clear a break with the Roman Catholic Church as the movements under Calvin and Luther. Its development was gradual and it sought to preserve what was deemed the best in the past tradition.

Former Justice Oliver Wendell Holmes is reported to have observed that in the nineteenth century mankind seemed to

have been on the threshold of an age of reason and that the
promise of an age of enlightenment attainable by man was
near at hand. Then came the twentieth century with its wars
and tyrannies and caused doubts and questions to arise in the
minds of thoughtful people as to whether or not man was a
reasonable being, capable of using for his well-being the knowledge and the discoveries of released power.

In order to answer this problem we need to consider a man
of the eighteenth century, Jonathan Edwards, who made a
profound contribution to the world's religious thought. He
is rightly placed high in the top ranks of American theologians
and philosophers. He was born on the fifth of October, 1703,
and was graduated as valedictorian from Yale in 1720. The
remainder of his life he spent in study, teaching, preaching
and the writing of books.

Edwards is popularly and mistakenly known to the twentieth century as a preacher of hell fire. The particular reason
for this belief probably is due to a single sermon preached in
Enfield, Connecticut, in July 1741, and entitled "Sinners in
the Hands of an Angry God." Edwards preached at other
times on this general theme, but this sermon was the most extreme and best remembered. The majority of his sermons,
however, proclaimed the will, the just love and peace of God
rather than damnation for mankind.

Jonathan Edwards' reputation as a philosopher and theologian is chiefly associated with his treatise on the *Will*, which
has been called "the one large contribution that America has
made to the deep philosophic thought of the world." This
treatise shows his utter devotion to God's will and his belief
that life is a struggle by man to know and do God's will. Certainly Edwards must be rated as one of the most able, if not
the most able of the religious thinkers of America, and as a
thinker he ranks with Augustine, Aquinas and Calvin.

Dr. Arthur Cushman McGiffert, Jr., concludes his book *From Jonathan Edwards* with the following statement:

Above all others of his own time he made a name for America at home and overseas. He still maintains his position as one of the most stimulating and forceful minds America has produced.[4]

A penniless immigrant boy who landed at Ellis Island in the later part of the last century was asked, "Do you have a friend in America?" "Yes," he replied, "Abraham Lincoln." To the everlasting credit of the immigration authorities the lad was admitted and became the great scholar and inventor, Michael Pupin.

On the twelfth day of February, 1809, in a log cabin in the backwoods of Kentucky, Abraham Lincoln was born. He exercised the great gift God gives to man, the gift of growth. He grew until he was acclaimed "the greatest American," and after his death Stanton said of him, "Now he belongs to the ages."

Throughout his mature years he sought to solve the great moral and economic problem which vexed this country—the problem of slavery. He became a prophet statesman, blending the righteousness of a prophet with the political sagacity of a statesman. Lincoln was convinced of the necessity of freedom if this nation is to endure. He said in a letter to H. L. Pierce in 1859: "Those who deny freedom to others deserve it not for themselves, and under a just God, cannot long retain it."

Justice ruled him as the North Star rules the compass. His was a justice predicated on integrity. Once some of his friends pleaded with him not to make a speech, predicting his defeat

---

[4] Arthur Cushman McGiffert, Jr., *From Jonathan Edwards* (New York and London, Harper & Brothers, 1932), p. 214. Reprinted by permission.

in the election if he did so. He replied, "If it should be decreed that I should go down to defeat because of this speech, then let me go down linked with truth." That is it: "linked with truth."

In the Gettysburg and Second Inaugural Addresses are found the utterances of one who knew the sore distress of humanity, and who also knew that "the judgments of the Lord are true and righteous all together." The words "With malice toward none; with charity for all; with firmness in the right, as God gives us to see the right, let us strive on to finish the work we are in." We who are living today in the midst of a world-wide epidemic of hatred need to heed these words.

Why ought we to desire to Lincolnize America? Primarily because he presents to us that sense of impartial justice so needed, but so lacking today—justice for the humble, justice for all, which can be won only as men take charge of their own lives and assume a worthy part in the creating of an honest and friendly world. He knew well what we ought to know, that "the end of complacency is the first step back to faith."

"By universal acknowledgment the foremost Christian statesman of the first half of this century was the late William Temple." This is the judgment of Dr. Henry P. Van Dusen. None who are well acquainted with the religious thought and life of the Protestant Church in the first half of the twentieth century will question this statement and none can successfully challenge its validity.

William Temple was born in 1881 and attended Rugby and Balliol College, and became a Fellow and Lecturer of Queen's College, Oxford. He wrote numerous articles and books, which had widespread influence. Of first rank was his book entitled *Nature, Man and God,* which was one of the greatest of the Gifford Lecture series. He lectured at Oxford,

Cambridge, Glasgow, Harvard and the University of Chicago. In 1929 he became Archbishop of York, and in 1942 the Archbishop of Canterbury, and remained in that post until his death in 1944.

According to Dr. Van Dusen: "Temple's towering eminence lay in the fact that in him superb natural gifts of mind and heart, illumined and disciplined by solid learning and wide experience, were permeated and ennobled by deep spirituality and unaffected simplicity."[5] William Temple was a giant in both the mental and spiritual realms. This great teacher, able theologian, ecumenical leader, was a five-talented man who used his talents to glorify God. He was a devout Christian who dedicated all his gifts to the service of man because he looked upon life as a commitment from God. Therefore, he was able to see the greatness of the opportunity of those dark, and yet bright times in which he lived, for he knew that man's "sufficiency is in God."

"How can we make Christianity naturalized in India, not a foreign thing, identified with a foreign government and a foreign people, but a part of the national life of India and contributing its power to India's uplift? What would you, as one of the Hindu leaders of India, tell me, a Christian, to do in order to make it possible?"[6]

This was the comprehensive question asked by Dr. E. Stanley Jones, who knew Gandhi personally and was closely associated with him for over forty years in India's struggle for freedom. The reply which Gandhi made to the question by Dr. Jones is revealing:

[5] Dr. Henry P. Van Dusen, *God in Education* (New York: Charles Scribner's Sons, 1951), p. 23. Reprinted by permission of the publishers.

[6] E. Stanley Jones, *Mahatma Gandhi—An Interpretation* (New York and Nashville, Abingdon-Cokesbury Press, 1948), p. 51. Reprinted by permission of the publishers.

First, I would suggest that all of you Christians, missionaries and all, must begin to live more like Jesus Christ. Second, practice your religion without adulterating it or toning it down. Third, emphasize love and make it your working force, for love is central in Christianity. Fourth, study the non-Christian religions more sympathetically to find the good that is within them, in order to have a more sympathetic approach to the people.[7]

Gandhi was a Hindu, not a Christian; nevertheless he often told of his indebtedness to the New Testament and especially to the teachings and life of Jesus. He said: "I read the New Testament to let the figure of Christ come through." In his thinking and life "he was one who followed Jesus the Prince of Peace, more closely than any man I know in the Twentieth Century," declared John Haynes Holmes in 1932 after he had met Gandhi in India.

Gandhi was described as "the greatest man in the world in the twentieth century." Was it because he did more than any other man in winning independence for India? No! Important as that was, that was not why he was great. When a journalist said to Gandhi, "Politics is my religion," Gandhi quickly replied, "Religion is my politics." He knew that the supreme battle of the modern world is not between nations or groups but "the battle between good and evil in the soul of man." In this age of power politics, when we are so dominated by things that we bow down and worship the golden calf, we need to understand that if life is to survive on this earth and have quality and worth it will not be in the struggle of men "red of tooth and claw," like animals around some jungle water hole, but it will be by the "soul force" gaining mastery over earth's pagan forces.

Paradoxical it is that this champion of nonviolence met death by violence early in February 1948. The man who

---

[7] *Ibid.*, pp. 51, 52.

loved even his enemies died at the hand of an enemy. Albert Einstein said of him: "Generations to come, it may be, will scarcely believe that such a one as this ever in flesh and blood walked upon this earth." What message does this "little man" have for our needy, headlong age?

First: "You Christians must begin to live more like Christ." To do this we must understand what Jesus meant when he said, "Follow me, and I will make you to become . . ." Often, in our worship of Christ we have been halfway people and neglected to follow him.

Second: "Practice your religion without adulterating it or toning it down." We need to heed that advice. We are prone to substitute secondary matters for primary religion as a way of life to be lived. Thus, "we have inoculated the world with a mild form of Christianity so that it is now proof against the real thing."

Third: "Emphasize love and make it your working force, for love is central in Christianity." His basic philosophy— *Satyagraha* or "soul force"—made love central in Christianity as an organized working force, a "truth force." He made the Cross operative in the political and economic as well as in the religious. This is a challenge to the whole war system. This principle of passive resistance and love worked for Gandhi, and he asked Christians to try it—organized love instead of organized force.

Fourth: "Study the non-Christian religions more sympathetically to find the good that is within them, in order to have a more sympathetic approach to the people." We Christians are too apt to approach other religions with a critical attitude, seeking for the bad in them, rather than for the good.

In these four principles we find the secret of this "little man's" powerful life. In his weakness he turned to God, and God put His strength behind Gandhi's weakness and made

him strong. When asked the secret of his power, Gandhi replied graphically:

A clean heart,
A clear conscience,
A cool head,
Regular communion with God,
Abstention from carnal food and pleasure,
No alcohol, smoking and condiments,
A strict vegetarian diet,
And love for all my fellow-men.

Gandhi's influence lives in many a Christian heart and in
many places throughout the world, for in him was recognized
a compelling embodiment of Christ's way of life and love. He
overcame evil with good and thus won "the victory that over-
cometh the world."

One man still living will I consider, and only one, and that
is Albert Schweitzer. He is probably the most gifted genius
of our age. He earned a Doctor's degree four times over—in
philosophy, in theology, in music and in medicine. In establishing the mission hospital at Lambarene, French Equatorial
Africa, in 1913, he began what proved to be his lifework.
Author of many books, he is noted for his ethical philosophy,
to which he gave the name "Reverence for Life," and for his
profound religious insights.

The twin graces, the grace of compassion and the grace of
gratitude, grew side by side in his life. They determined his
whole attitude and were the foundation of his ethical philosophy and religious motivation; they shaped his career in the
fields both of thought and action.

We need an understanding of the core of his philosophy and
theology which is "reverence for life"—for all life. The origin
of this concept is best expressed in his *Memories of Childhood
and Youth*. No doubt he received the clue to this idea from
Goethe, who proclaimed that the key to religion and the good

life is reverence for everything within man and surrounding man, a reverence for the basic Reality of the Cosmos. In Schweitzer's book one follows the growth of this idea in a child who refused to kill birds and animals as his classmates did, and did not participate in teasing unfortunate persons in the village in which they lived. The statue of a Negro in Colmar made a marked impression upon him and led him to dedicate his life to helping heal the bodies and souls of the natives who lived in Africa's wilderness.

In July 1949, Dr. Schweitzer made his first visit to America, to deliver the principal addresses at Aspen, Colorado, on the occasion of the two hundredth anniversary of Goethe's birth. This celebration was characterized by Robert M. Hutchins, chairman of the United States Goethe Bicentennial Foundation, as "the greatest cultural event ever held in the United States." On this journey across "the strange and friendly land, America," Dr. Schweitzer stopped in Chicago to receive an honorary degree from the University of Chicago and to give a concert on the great organ in Rockefeller Chapel of that University. On both occasions crowds jammed the huge chapel to hear and to see this gifted minister, philosopher, physician and musician. His edition of Bach's organ works is a standard musical text and his biography of Bach is unsurpassed, as is his knowledge of the organ, both as to its structure and to technique in playing it.

He is a doctor of medicine whose thirty-eight years of selfless devotion to natives of French Equatorial Africa are "bright highlights in the relations between the white race and the black." He forgot himself into world-wide recognition because he took at its face value Jesus' statement: "He that loses his life shall find it."

He is a philosopher who, like Schopenhauer, to whom he owes much, is critical of our civilization and believes it bears in itself the seeds of its own destruction. Yet his interpretation of Schopenhauer's "will to live" does not result in futile resignation, but in devotion to all life and all of life. Like Spengler and Toynbee he has probed deeply into the ills of our sick world and made a diagnosis that is not superficial but which requires deep surgery if civilization is to have a chance to recover from its decline.

He is a Protestant minister who follows the Great Physician in "going about doing good." He is a biblical scholar whose historical criticism of the New Testament in the early part of this century caused great controversy in the circle of scholar and clergyman.

Schweitzer went to Africa because he felt a sense of deep obligation to those who did not have the things he enjoyed in a physical, mental and spiritual sense. There he has lived a life not of sacrifice but of privilege. In that strange land he thought deeply and came to have a profound respect for all living creatures, hence his cosmic reverence for life.

This reverence for life came out of his study of and devotion to Jesus Christ. In his book *The Quest of the Historical Jesus* he concludes with these words:

He [Jesus] comes to us as One unknown, without a name, as of old, by the lake-side, He came to those men who knew Him not. He speaks to us the same word: "Follow thou me!" and sets us to the tasks which He has to fulfil for our time. He commands. And to those who obey Him, be they wise or simple, He will reveal Himself in the toils, the conflicts, the sufferings which they shall pass through in His fellowship, and, as an ineffable mystery, they shall learn in their own experience Who He is.

Albert Schweitzer richly deserves the recognition the world has given him, and the wide acclaim—"the greatest living Christian."

These are but a few of the heroes of the faith who made their telling witness. Thousands of others, many unnumbered and unknown, also bore their witness to Christ.

Who follows in their train?

FOUR PILLARS OF THE PROTESTANT FAITH

THERE are two main roads which religious faith may travel. One is the road of an infallible external authority; the other is by inner experience and investigation of the Scriptures and life. The first leads along a highway traveled through many centuries; the other also travels old roads but is prone to push out into new ways, thus enabling the comrades of the quest to seek for new truth. Often the roads converge, but always they proceed by different means and toward different ends, for to a large extent the means employed determine the end.

The Roman Catholic faith follows the former of these routes. It rests its religious beliefs on the authority of the Church, affirms the infallibility of its past pronouncements and zealously endeavors to preserve them unbroken. Through its Pope and priests it interprets the Scriptures for its adherents, prescribes what they shall believe and discourages all deviations from the established path. This naturally produces a type of thought which exerts a powerful influence toward the maintenance of the status quo; little or no opportunity is left for progress toward a more rational faith, with the result that the Church tends to become priest-ridden and static.

Protestantism owes its origin to a remonstrance against the authority of the Church and to its insistence on the right of each individual to think his own thoughts, read his own Bible, find his own way to God and make his witness of the

Gospel without the mediation of priest or Mass. This insistence led to the formulation of several basic principles by the leaders of the Reformation. We shall call them "Four Pillars of the Protestant Faith." They are: "The Priesthood of All Believers," "The Just Shall Live by Faith," "The Right of Private Judgment" and "The Authority of the Bible."

It is first necessary to consider the doctrine of apostolic succession held by the Roman Catholic Church in order to appraise rightly these "Four Pillars of the Protestant Faith." This doctrine taught that every priest at the time when he is ordained receives, by the "laying on of hands," the authority of Christ himself, which had first been conferred in a peculiar sense on Peter. The structure of the Roman Church, as has already been mentioned, rests primarily on the interpretation which it makes of a single text of the Bible. "Thou art Peter," Jesus is reported to have said, "and upon this rock I will build my church." The verbal authenticity of this text is open to question. But even so, let us take the statement as it stands and examine it. The Roman Church declares that *petra* (meaning *rock*) refers to Petros (Peter) and that Christ therefore said he would build his church on Peter. Scholars have pointed out that there are no other texts or parts of the New Testament to support this text or corroborate this interpretation. Furthermore, James, not Peter, was the outstanding figure in the Jerusalem church.

Because of this doctrine of apostolic succession, the Roman Catholic Church claims that every one of its priests stands in an unbroken succession of authority back to Christ himself, and that outside of this historic succession no one has Christ's authority or is able to represent him.

The leaders of the Protestant Reformation challenged the validity of this basis of priestly authority for two reasons: one, they were disturbed because too many priests were most un-Christlike. In fact, the spirit, attitude and practices of

many of the priests were in direct contrast to those of Jesus.
John Tetzel, a priest in the Roman Church, was assigned the
task of raising money through the sale of indulgences as a
commission man of the Fugger banking house. It has been
facetiously said that it might be easier to trace the apostolic
succession of such men as Tetzel through Judas than through
Peter. Anyhow, the unbroken succession of "laying on of
hands" certainly never guaranteed spiritual succession.

The second and primary reason for challenging priestly
authority was that searchers of the Scriptures refuted the
claim and proclaimed a new doctrine: namely, the priesthood
of all believers. The conflict between the priests and the
prophets is of long standing. In both the Old and the New
Testaments is told the story of priests both good and bad.
For example, the ancient story of Eli in First Samuel
speaks favorably of him as a priest. In the New Testament
(Luke 1:5-80) is told the story of Zacharias, who was a
priest of good deeds. In most cases, however, the priest plays
the role of a villain as the champion of corruption and the
enemy of righteousness. As we read the prophets, Isaiah,
Amos and Hosea, we see the priests as defenders of a harmful religious system arrayed against the prophets, who are
God's ambassadors and defenders of man's right and dignity.
The word *prophet* means not a foreteller in the sense of a fortune teller, but one who forth tells of the will of God. The
prophet is the medium through whom God speaks to man.

Over against the great messages of ethical righteousness of
the Old Testament prophets are the rites and ceremonies of
the priests used as pious masks to hide their sins of lust and
greed. This provoked the ire of the prophets, and with holy
boldness they exposed the corrupt practices in the temples and
places of worship, the lustful festivity and the widespread dis-
honesty which brought rich gains to the priests and money-
changers. As prophets they proclaimed a twofold message:

the righteousness of God and a concern for man and his right relationship with his fellow men.

Jesus was drastic in his denunciation of those who worked against God's righteousness and he accused them of dealing in things of little or no worth to man's well-being. He said (Matthew 23:23-24):

Woe unto you, scribes and Pharisees, hypocrites! for ye pay tithe of mint and anise and cummin, and have omitted the weightier matters of the law, judgment, mercy and faith: these ought ye to have done, and not to leave the other undone. Ye blind guides, which strain at a gnat, and swallow a camel.

This general principle Jesus illustrated in concrete terms, as is evidenced by the direct action he took against the money-changers in the temple (Matthew 21:12-13):

And Jesus went into the temple of God, and cast out all them that sold and bought in the temple, and overthrew the tables of the moneychangers, and the seats of them that sold doves, And said unto them, It is written, My house shall be called the house of prayer; but ye have made it a den of thieves.

Equally severe was Jesus' condemnation of those who made a pretext of religion to cover up their nefarious motives. He called them what they were—hypocrites. Listen to his incriminating denunciation as it is found in the twenty-third chapter of Matthew from the thirteenth verse on. For example, Matthew 23:13-14, 25-28 and 33:

But woe unto you, scribes and Pharisees, hypocrites! for ye shut up the kingdom of heaven against men: for ye neither go in yourselves, neither suffer ye them that are entering to go in. Woe unto you, scribes and Pharisees, hypocrites! for ye devour widows' houses, and for a pretence make long prayer: therefore ye shall receive the greater damnation. . . .

Woe unto you, scribes and Pharisees, hypocrites! for ye make clean the outside of the cup and of the platter, but within they are full of extortion and excess. Thou blind Pharisee, cleanse first that which is within the cup and platter, that the outside of them may be clean also. Woe unto you, scribes and Pharisees, hypocrites! for ye are like unto whited sepulchres, which indeed appear beautiful outward, but are within full of dead men's bones, and of all uncleanness. Even so ye are full of hypocrisy and iniquity. . . .

Ye serpents, ye generation of vipers, how can ye escape the damnation of hell?

St. Paul also brought vigorous charges against the priests who perverted religion. He claimed that the good news of the love and grace of God, which frees men from the slavish and corrupting confines of a legalistic system of law, could not be proclaimed through the petty and unworthy beliefs and practices of the priests. The really essential things were being left out and there remained only a caricature of the original idea which was supposed to have been furthered by religious practices. Read again Paul's words in Galatians, particularly the fifth chapter, verses 1-6, 13-14, 16 and 18-23:

Stand fast therefore in the liberty wherewith Christ hath made us free, and be not entangled again with the yoke of bondage. Behold, I Paul say unto you, that if ye be circumcised, Christ shall profit you nothing. For I testify again to every man that is circumcised, that he is a debtor to do the whole law. Christ is become of no effect unto you, whosoever of you are justified by the law; ye are fallen from grace. For we through the Spirit wait for the hope of righteousness by faith. For in Jesus Christ neither circumcision availeth any thing, nor uncircumcision; but faith which worketh by love. . . .

For, brethren, ye have been called unto liberty; only use not liberty for an occasion to the flesh, but by love serve one another. For all the law is fulfilled in one word, even in this; Thou shalt love thy neighbor as thyself. . . .

This I say then, Walk in the Spirit, and ye shall not fulfil the lust of the flesh. . . . But if ye be led of the Spirit, ye are not under the law. Now the works of the flesh are manifest, which are these; Adultery, fornication, uncleanness, lasciviousness, idolatry, witchcraft, hatred, variance, emulations, wrath, strife, seditions, heresies, envyings, murders, drunkenness, revellings, and such like: of the which I tell you before, as I have also told you in time past, that they which do such things shall not inherit the kingdom of God. But the fruit of the Spirit, is love, joy, peace, longsuffering, gentleness, goodness, faith, meekness, temperance: against such there is no law.

Read these same ideas even more directly stated in Romans and ponder over these words of Paul's as found in the seventh and eighth chapters:

For the good that I would I do not: but the evil which I would not, that I do. Now if I do that I would not, it is no more I that do it, but sin that dwelleth in me. I find then a law, that, when I would do good, evil is present with me. For I delight in the law of God after the inward man: But I see another law in my members, warring against the law of my mind, and bringing me into captivity to the law of sin which is in my members. O wretched man that I am! who shall deliver me from the body of this death?

For if ye live after the flesh, ye shall die: but if ye through the Spirit do mortify the deeds of the body, ye shall live. For as many as are led by the Spirit of God, they are the sons of God. For ye have not received the spirit of bondage again to fear; but ye have received the Spirit of adoption, whereby we cry, Abba, Father. The Spirit itself beareth witness with our spirit, that we are the children of God: And if children, then heirs; heirs of God, and joint-heirs with Christ; if so be that we suffer with him, that we may be also glorified together. . . .

For I am persuaded, that neither death, nor life, nor angels, nor principalities, nor powers, nor things present, nor things to come, Nor height, nor depth, nor any other creature, shall be able to separate us from the love of God, which is in Christ Jesus our Lord.

The Reformers of the sixteenth century went back to the Bible, and although their statements of the principles reveal some slight differences, yet without exception they agree on the need of faith in God and the availability of God as essential to salvation. Luther, Calvin and Knox, all realized that there was great need of reform in the Church of their own time. They were moved by the living spirit of Christ to do something about it. They did not have any thought of starting a new church, but it was their earnest desire to change some of the misconceptions and do away with the corruption which they saw in the Church. They endeavored to put the proper emphasis on the ideas and methods that were of real value so that the people would know of the love of God as revealed in Jesus Christ and so that their belief would become a vital force in their lives.

Recorded in the Bible are many instances of the sensitiveness of man to God's will and purpose. Isaiah, after offering many excuses exclaimed: "Here am I, send me." Amos proclaimed: "The Lord God hath spoken, who can but prophesy?" Paul, captive to the spirit and purpose of Christ, cried out, "Woe is me if I preach not the gospel!" As the ancient prophets were sensitive to the will of God, so were Paul and the Reformers. Martin Luther was moved by the same power that possessed Isaiah, Amos and Paul, and his popularly quoted words, "Here I stand, I can do no other, so help me God!" have helped to keep men on their feet. When John Knox answered the scornful question of Mary Queen of Scots: "What are you in this commonwealth?" by saying, "God has made me a profitable member," his declaration also grew out of heroic convictions and resulted in a positive affirmation of faith rather than in actual protest. Conflict with the established church came as a result of the relentless witness of the Reformers. They defined and reaffirmed the essential nature of Christian teaching and life, because they were convinced that spiritual truths and values had been neglected. This led to the formulating of convictions which afterward became known by the terms which described the nature of the doctrine proclaimed.

Each of the Four Pillars of the Protestant Faith is an important affirmation. These principles must be considered for two reasons: first, that we may know and comprehend their historic value; second, that their worth to us as Protestants living in the last half of the twentieth century may be known, understood and fully appreciated.

THE PRIESTHOOD OF ALL BELIEVERS

Probably the doctrine most misunderstood by both Roman Catholics and Protestants, and most neglected by Protestants, is the priesthood of all believers. It affirms that every man is God's minister, that each person is his own priest, *but with a social responsibility;* therefore, each person is his brother's priest. This does not mean, as the Roman Catholic Church and some Protestants say it does, that every man is free to believe and do as he pleases, that "every man is his own priest." The emphasis on the direct access of man to God and on the inescapable responsibility he has to God and his fellow men is only a part of this misunderstood doctrine. The fuller and truer meaning is that every man is his own priest only insofar as he belongs to the "mutual ministry of all believers." In the fellowship of believers he is united "in the communion of the forgiven and forgiving."

The Protestant clergyman in the light of this principle is only another "believer." There is a parity between "believers" in the pulpit and the pew. Yet it is recognized that not all men and women in the fellowship have those qualities of mind and spirit which enable them to be "ministers of the gospel" in its more restricted sense—ordained clergymen. The

Protestant clergyman conducts public worship, interprets the Scriptures and administers the sacraments in a representative capacity for the fellowship. Luther stated it clearly:

[All believers] are worthy to appear before God, to pray for others, to teach each other mutually the things that are of God—so ought we freely to help our neighbors by our body and our works, and each should become to the other a sort of Christ, so that we may be mutually Christ's, and that the same Christ may be in all of us.

Luther further declared:

Let everyone who knows himself to be a Christian be assured of this, and apply it to himself, that we are all priests, and there is no difference between us. . . . As many as have been baptized are all equally priests.

Calvin rejected the idea that there is a difference between the clergy and laity. He declared, "All of God's people are his clergy"; that is, all believers are priests.

These pronouncements were based on the words found in the First Epistle of Peter 2:5:

Ye also . . . are built up a spiritual house, an holy priesthood, to offer up spiritual sacrifices, acceptable to God by Jesus Christ.

In Paul's First Epistle to the Corinthians are these words:

Now ye are the body of Christ, and members in particular. And God hath set some in the church, first apostles, secondarily prophets, thirdly teachers, after that miracles, then gifts of healings, helps, governments, diversities of tongues. Are all apostles? are all prophets? are all teachers? are all workers of miracles?

As Luther said, "As many of us as have been baptized are all equally priests."

The priesthood of all believers means their participation as intelligent and responsible citizens in the government of their church. Thus the principle of representative government was established in both Church and State. This principle holds that every Christian has a sacred calling. The ministry or the priesthood is not degraded to the secular level. Rather by the belief that all worthy vocations are blessed by God, the life and work of every Christian is lifted to the sacred level.

Christ is the only high priest for every true believer (Hebrews 4:14). Any man can seek God and find Him and be found of Him. Forgiveness and reconciliation are a direct relationship between a man and God and do not require the intervention of a human priest.

What is really most important in the doctrine of the priesthood of all believers is not that it denies clericalism, but that it affirms the duty of all Christians, by the fact that they belong to the priesthood of faith, to serve one another. Thus the Church comes into being as the fellowship of believers in Christ, who both hear the Word of God and follow it. The principle of the "priesthood of all believers" relates not only to the rights but also to the obligations of each believer. It requires that every Christian shall be a priest to his fellow men, helping them to know and understand the truth of God as revealed in Jesus Christ. It also means that every Christian must be a coworker with God, that His will of justice, righteousness and peace may be established on earth.

"Faith in God," when it is realized in its full and real meaning, is always coupled with good works. Yet man is not "working for credit." Each person may enter into a filial relationship with God, his Father and our Father also. It is then that his life becomes meaningful as he is a co-operator, a coworker with God. With Augustine he can truly say, "Love

God and do as you please," for then his sole aim is to please God.

When rightly understood, the doctrine of the priesthood of all believers gives to the ordinary man a dignity and understanding which are matched in no other teaching. It places a new value on the common life and labor as it rejects the division between the "religious" life and the "secular" life.

Recently I was traveling by automobile through the central part of Illinois. Much of the land on either side of the road had been freshly plowed, and the soil appeared very black. I remarked to the modern-trained farmer with whom I was riding, "How black that dirt is!"

The farmer replied, "That isn't dirt; that is earth—the good earth." True, dirt is only earth out of place.

The early Catholic Church did a great disservice to mankind in dividing the world into sacred and secular. The Protestant holds that all honest work, which serves the children of God, is sacred in the sight of God. Luther said that it is more important for a Christian to serve his neighbor than to renounce the world and embrace the life of a monk. This is in essence the teachings of Romans 12:6-8:

Having then gifts differing according to the grace that is given to us, whether prophecy, let us prophesy according to the proportion of faith; Or ministry, let us wait on our ministering: or he that teacheth, on teaching; Or he that exhorteth, on exhortation: he that giveth, let him do it with simplicity; he that ruleth, with diligence; he that sheweth mercy, with cheerfulness.

All do not have the same gifts, but each has the responsibility of using God's gifts to the fullest extent. God has entrusted to each one of us a talent. Use it or lose it! We need to know with Moses that "the place whereon thou standest is holy ground." As Mrs. Browning so well expresses it,

Earth's crammed with heaven,
And every common bush afire with God;
And only he who sees takes off his shoes—
The rest sit round it and pluck blackberries . . .[1]

THE JUST SHALL LIVE BY FAITH

Another cardinal principle of the Protestant Reformation
was "justification by faith," from Paul's: "The just shall live
by faith" (Romans 1:17). As the Protestant leaders studied
their New Testaments, especially the words of Jesus and Paul,
and as they read the works of the Church Fathers, particularly
Augustine, they came to the basic conclusion that one could
not gain the favor of God by "good works." They held that
everyone has the favor of God, and that to be a Christian one
has to have faith in God and accept His great gifts and use
them aright. Therefore, any attempt to purchase God's favor
is an attempt on the part of man to limit God and abuse His
power. The foundation of the Protestant faith, first and foremost, is the primacy of the sovereignty of God. God, not man,
is sovereign. God is free. We are free in the priesthood of
believers because we believe in a free God.

The central affirmation of Protestant Christianity concerns
not man but God. It proclaims the sovereignty of God. God,
the Creator and Redeemer, is not bound. He is not confined
to limited forms of life, i.e., to historically relative, man-made
institutions, for example Roman Catholic hierarchalism.
Protestant faith and life arise from the hearing of the speaking God who discloses himself when and how he chooses, and
calls men into fellowship with himself. The church, therefore,
is a communion of believers, a *people* committed to God be-

---

[1] From Elizabeth Barrett Browning's "Aurora Leigh," in *Masterpieces of
Religious Verse* (New York, Harper & Brothers, 1948). Reprinted by permission.

cause he has chosen them. It is *not an institution* of a super-personal character.[2]

The whole conception of salvation by means of a system of bargaining through the priest with God is out of harmony with the New Testament teaching. God does not bargain with men, He is Lord over the Church and over history. Such a system of bondage was like that from which Paul sought release. He contrasts his frustration and desperate endeavor to find salvation through the "law" (a system of good works) with his glorious release after finding "faith" in Christ and his Gospel. As Luther reread and studied his New Testament, he found in Paul a kindred soul, whose experience closely paralleled his own. It became evident to Luther that the Roman Catholic Church believed not in the Christian doctrine of "justification by faith," but rather in a system of "works" both good and bad. This belief fitted better into that Church's system of penance and indulgences. The Protestant holds that reconciliation with God is not gained by any legalistic formula set up for man by the Church. It is the gift of God.

For God so loved the world, that he gave his only begotten Son, that whosoever believeth in him should not perish, but have everlasting life (John 3:16).

Man needs only to accept God's grace in faith and repentance. Good works do not save man; they are the fruits of men who are saved.

To Paul, salvation meant much more than escape from, or a shortening of the period of suffering in purgatory. Salvation is more than the negative being saved from death: it is

---

2 Wilhelm Pauck, *The Heritage of the Reformation* (Glencoe, Illinois, The Free Press, 1950), p. 149. Reprinted by permission of the publishers.

the positive being saved for life. Salvation means the recognition of the great truth as stated in First John 3 :2 :

Beloved, now are we the sons of God, and it doth not yet appear what we shall be : but we know that, when he shall appear, we shall be like him; for we shall see him as he is.

The reason why Reformers broke with Rome is clearly evident in their conception of the Christian life. Rome taught that in order to enter upon the Christian life, one must do, or have done for one, certain things that made possible the acquisition of a new nature. The Reformers affirmed that the way to enter into the Christian life was through an act of personal trust that brought one into the right relationship with God.

This doctrine of justification by faith is a way of saying in technical language what Jesus said much more simply when he talked about the childlike spirit. It comprises two beliefs about the Christian life which give distinctive quality to the Protestant position : First, it is so wonderful and lofty that man can do nothing for himself to earn it, but must be content to receive it as the gift of God; second, it is so adapted to man's true nature that to enter on it he requires no miraculous change of nature, but only an act of trust which is itself the gift of God. The Protestant asserts that man needs only a change of relationship.

Dr. Daniel Day Williams, in the first chapter of his revealing book, *God's Grace and Man's Hope,* states :

"Neo-orthodoxy" is a term which points to that widespread movement in contemporary Protestant theology which seeks to recover the central theme of the Reformation : justification by faith in the redemption wrought by God in Jesus Christ, as the foundation of the Christian Gospel and of the Church. The three names which probably stand out most

prominently when we think of this movement are Karl Barth,
Emil Brunner, and Reinhold Niebuhr, not only because they
are among its leaders, but because their writings are most
widely known. Certainly there are important differences . . .
among them. . . . Here, however, I shall run the risk of treating the standpoint as a whole. My thesis is that all the neo-
orthodox thinkers neglect a fundamental Christian insight
into the meaning of life within the grace of God. They overlook it in different ways, but they all overlook it.[3]

In the last chapter of his book, Dr. Williams further contends:

We need not make an artificial separation between justification by faith as the receiving of the gift of forgiveness, and
regeneration as the actual beginning of the new life. There is
no such separation, as Calvin himself takes great pains to
make clear.[4]

The Protestant is convinced that by faith alone is one able
to be saved. Faith is an absolute reliance upon God and a
complete trust in Him as He is made known through Jesus.
Sin, therefore, to the Protestant, is the rebellion of man
against God leading to separation from God. This results
in a tension between God and man, which is only remedied
by God's act of forgiveness. In complete reliance on God and
not on himself, the Protestant proclaims the freedom of the
Christian man. This principle is related to the doctrine of
the priesthood of all believers, for everyone who has come
under the lordship of God through faith in the gospel of
Jesus Christ is thereby a free man, subject to God alone, and
therefore is a priest. Thus the Roman distinction between

---

[3] Daniel Day Williams, *God's Grace and Man's Hope* (New York, Harper
& Brothers, 1949), p. 27. Reprinted by permission of the publishers.
[4] *Ibid.*, p. 188.

priest and layman is destroyed. The Reformers labored for the reformation of Christianity by rejecting Roman Catholic power in the name and spirit of the Christian faith.

The charge that the Protestant faith is wholly individualistic is not true. Those who persist in speaking of the "Protestant individualism" of Luther, Calvin and others, betray their ignorance. Luther and Calvin and the other great leaders were not "peevish little individuals shut up in the dungeons of their own subjectivism." Even a meager understanding of Faith reveals that it is intensely personal and more, that it is also the source of a relationship of unselfish love for all men. It is, therefore, never completely individualistic.

The statement that "faith without works is dead," presupposes that good works must necessarily follow faith. Faith without ethical consequences is a lie. God does not need our sacrifices, but He has, nevertheless, appointed a representative to receive them, namely our neighbor.

THE RIGHT OF PRIVATE JUDGMENT

The third principle of the Reformation was "the right of private judgment," the right of every Christian to follow the dictates of his own conscience, the moral sense that helps him to determine the difference between right and wrong, in matters of faith and practice. Primarily the religion of the Roman Church was a religion of dogma, duties and restrictions. The Protestant revolt against this system was an assertion of human rights and freedom. For years the Roman Catholic Church had imposed conformity of thought and action upon man. Everyone was told what he could and must believe. In matters of religion he was told: "Thou shalt not think."

Granted, freedom is a dangerous thing; it is more dangerous than anything else in the world—except lack of freedom. The Reformers went back to Jesus for their authority in all matters. So must we. The Reformation did not begin with Luther; it began with Jesus Christ. Jesus, in speaking of the professional religious leaders of his day, said: " . . . they bind heavy burdens and grievous to be borne, and lay them on men's shoulders; but they themselves will not move them with one of their fingers" (Matthew 23:4). Again to the Jews he said, "And ye shall know the truth, and the truth shall make you free" (John 8:32). Paul's Epistle to the Galatians is his declaration of independence on their behalf.

The teaching of Jesus stresses the dignity of man. He invariably contended that persons are of more value than institutions. "The Sabbath was made for man, and not man for the Sabbath" (Mark 2:27). Here is exposed the institutional fallacy that man can be used as a means to serve institutional ends. Persons are themselves the ends to be served, and institutions are always the means. Democracy rests on a religious foundation and cannot exist without it. Human worth is spiritual; it is predicated on this relationship with God. Man is the child of God. This explains man's capacity to be a creature of infinite worth.

To be free, one cannot enslave another. As Lincoln rightly contended, "No man has the right to enslave another man without that man's consent." He stated the same principle in another way in his debate with Douglas at Galesburg, Illinois: "They are blowing out the moral lights who contend that slavery is right." He was thinking of a system of slavery in America, but the principle he stated had universal application. He further stated this principle in a positive way:

As I would not be a slave, so I would not be a master. This expresses my idea of democracy. Whatever differs from this, to the extent of the difference, is no democracy.

It is a healthy democracy that is immune to the communist or the Fascist bacteria. Protestantism believes that the most

effective antitoxin to dictatorship abroad is life-giving democracy at home. A society where impartial justice is practiced is the basic defense against all forms of tyranny. We
know that Stalin cannot be stopped by saluting Franco. The
Lambeth Conference said: "Communism has to be *outlived,*
not merely *outfought*."

On the first of November, 1950, the Pope, surrounded by
36 cardinals, 480 archbishops and bishops, and facing a
congregation estimated at nearly 200,000, made a statement
in regard to the Assumption of Mary for which infallibility
was claimed. Its importance may be measured by the fact that
it was the first time a Pope had spoken ex cathedra since the
dogma of Papal infallibility was promulgated in 1870. Dr.
Robert J. McCracken, Minister of the Riverside Church,
preached an excellent sermon on the Dogma of the Assumption of Mary on November 12, 1950. This sermon, which is
available in pamphlet form, states in a friendly but frank manner Dr. McCracken's reasons why it is impossible for the
intelligent Christian to accept the Dogma of the Assumption
of Mary. There is no historical or biblical evidence for it. In
order to accept this dogma we must sacrifice our right of
private judgment, and put out the light of reason which God
has entrusted to each one of us.

Protestant proclamation of "the right of private judgment"
puts the sanctity of the individual conscience above submission to external authority. It puts the individual's welfare
beyond the reach of all human tyranny and makes him a free
man. The extension of this principle of "the right of private
judgment" has been made manifest in the organization of
the Protestant churches around democratic ideas and ideals.
The form of ecclesiastical government is determined by the
people, whether Episcopal, Presbyterian or Congregational.
Protestant bishops and officers are elected by the people
through their representatives. Protestant judicial bodies are

constituted by the people, and their laws are adopted by the people. Protestant executives are responsible to the people. Protestant finances are managed by the people. Protestants know the truth of the statement made by Lord Acton, a Roman Catholic nobleman, that: "all power corrupts and absolute power corrupts absolutely," that it will corrupt a church as well as a state, a bishop as well as a businessman, and so Protestants keep power in the hands of the people. The people and the clergy hold power together with the majority control in the hands of the laity. The people promise to follow their spiritual leaders only "insofar as we see them follow Christ."

Protestants fear that a man who takes his religion from an "authoritarian Church" may be so conditioned that he will take his politics from an "authoritarian party," or his economics from an "authoritarian class." This is not a groundless fear as anyone who is acquainted with conditions in Spain, Italy and Mexico well knows. That is why Protestants insist that a free man's church should be governed by democratic principles. Protestantism calls on free men to build a better society than dictatorship can ever build, a society in which the sacredness of personality is recognized and everyone finds opportunity for the fullest self-expression of which he is capable.

Whenever Protestantism has been the dominant religious faith of the people, the free mind, free education and the democratic way have prevailed. Literacy is high in all the great Protestant nations. They are leaders in such social advances as old-age pensions, unemployment insurance and other movements for the well-being of the people. Protestantism, by insuring the free mind, has made people ready to withstand the impact of systems of the unfree mind. It calls for a society at once free and moral, democratic and just, both political and ecclesiastical.

THE AUTHORITY OF THE BIBLE

The Word of God is the language of God to man in "the divine-human encounter." Theology in the Reformation heritage concerns the Word of God in a dual sense: the Bible, which is the *record* of the Word of God; the confessional, which is the *response* to the Word of God. The two are complementary. Both revelation and response are required. Revelation is incomplete without response, and response is impossible without revelation.

The authority regarding the Word of God is, for the heirs of the Reformation, the Scriptures of the Old and New Testaments. The Bible is clearly the product of history and of men who are a part of that history. It is a record of the religious and political events of the descendants of Abraham. But the Bible is more than the history of man's relationship with man. It is the chief witness of Israel's dynamic encounter with God. "The Bible," says Philip Shaff in his *Creeds of Christendom,* "is the Word of God to man; the creed is man's answer to God."

That the Bible played a most significant part in the Protestant Reformation is an obvious fact. The statement that "the Bible and the Bible alone is the religion of Protestants and the seat of their authority," contains much truth. However, we must clarify the meaning of words like *Protestant, Bible* and *Authority.* As we have seen, the word *Protestant* comes from the word *protestari,* meaning "to profess, bear witness, declare openly." This is the meaning that is clearly reflected in the significant use of it at the Diet of Speyer in 1529:

We must protest in matters which concern God's honor, and the salvation and eternal life of our souls; everyone must stand and give account before God for himself, and no one can excuse himself by the action or decision of another, whether less or more.

This is a positive declaration of definite truths.

The question of authority is so central to the understanding of the nature and meaning of human life in general that it is necessary to examine the word *Bible* carefully. When Protestants say, "Here is the final authority in which right and power are united," they mean the Bible, as the authoritative Word of God. The Roman Church regards the Church as the authority in matters of doctrine and conduct. In the pre-Reformation days, instead of endeavoring to interpret the Bible to her people, the Roman Church made her elaborate system of doctrine a substitute for the Scriptures. The perversions and corruptions of Christian teachings made by the Church went on for centuries almost unchallenged. The rebellion finally came through such men as Luther, who, as priests, were able to read the Scriptures for themselves and could not avoid seeing the glaring contrasts between the real teaching of Scripture and the teaching and practices of the Roman Church.

It is often said that the Reformation simply substituted an infallible Bible for an infallible Pope, a formula which is incorrect on both counts. The popes were not generally regarded as infallible before the Reformation, and the Reformation did not acknowledge an infallible Bible. The Reformers simply asserted the traditional Christian conception that the Word of God in the Bible must be the last court of resort in the church. They applied this criterion more radically, to be sure, to widespread abuses than had been done before. The fundamental novelty with regard to the problem of authority which the sixteenth century produced was the new and unprecedented decision rendered by the Council of Trent. This was the council which gathered to reorganize the Roman church in defense against the Reformation just four hundred years ago. So radical was its reorganization that one may well ask the modern Romanist, "Where was your church before Trent?" To the dismay of its more sober members, the Council of Trent, for the first time in Christian history, set up "tradition" as of "equal" authority to the Bible.[5]

The Reformers rejected the authority of the Roman Catholic Church and the Pope and based their authority on the Bible. In it the progressive revelation of God is evidenced through the guidance and judgment of Jehovah on the life of Israel, as it is recorded in the Old Testament, and the redeeming love of God culminating in the life and teaching of Jesus found in the New Testament. Over against an "infallible church," which had become an apostate church, they placed an "infallible Bible." To be sure, the Roman Catholic Church recognized the authority of the Bible, but only when it was interpreted by an "infallible church." Like Protestants, the Catholics regard the Bible as the primary source of revelation. But they hold that the Bible apart from the Church cannot be rightly understood. To say that the use of the Bible by their laymen is not encouraged by the Roman Church is no longer true. But the Bible is too often a lawbook to which the Roman Catholic goes for information as to the constitution which God has given to his Church, and the laws which should regulate its activities. Like every lawbook, it requires an interpreter and the Roman Catholics claim that God has provided this interpreter in the hierarchy of the Church.

The priesthood, as the Roman Catholic conceives it, is not only the guardian of divine truth, but the channel of divine grace. The Protestant answer to this is the principle of the "right of private judgment" which demands that the search for spiritual truth should be conducted by minister

---

[5] James Hastings Nichols, *Primer for Protestants* (New York, Association Press, 1947), p. 62. Reprinted by permission of the publishers.

28/6/

and layman with the same zeal and honest attitude of mind used by the scientist in his search for scientific truth.

The acceptance of the Bible as the unquestionable authority of Protestants led to many differences of opinion as to what it taught. Because those who held the varying opinions believed that they were correct interpretations of biblical authority, each opinion was asserted as the authoritative teaching of Scripture. This resulted in an abuse which is the direct opposite of the end anticipated, for instead of bringing the opinions of men under the control and authority of Scripture, the authority of Scripture was actually claimed in support of human opinions. So human opinions were often set forth and believed as the "Word of God."

When the doctrine of verbal inspiration of the Bible, claimed by many of the early Protestants in their contest with an infallible Pope, is applied to the Bible in a literal sense and without discrimination, only confusion results. To contend that every word and phrase of the Bible "from cover to cover" is equally the inspired and authoritative message of God is to make it a dead book. So conceived, it takes an infallible church (of which there is none) to interpret the Bible. This view leaves no place for the progressive development of the Bible.

The Bible is not a book of magic, nor is it to be worshiped. The Bible is to be read, not as a manual of science, philosophy and ethics, but as an account which traces in words of unvarnished truth the specific dealings of men with the living God. The record of God's communication to man about the attaining of life abundant and eternal is in the Bible. The Bible views the history of the Hebrew people, the life of Jesus and the life of the Church as sharing in one continuous working of God in which every aspect of human life has its necessary and fruitful role to play. The Bible is the moving record of an expanding religious experience which culminated

Lincoln Christian College

in Jesus. His character and teaching, his life and his death, are the vital issues by which all the rest of the Bible must always be approached. It tells us of Jesus Christ, of what he said and did and does. It gives to us the deepest truths about the universe and human destiny.

In some sense the authoritativeness of the Bible has been claimed by nearly all Christendom. But the pertinent question arises: who is to interpret the Scripture? Rome answers: Only the hierarchy with the Pope, and in the light of the Fathers, so far as they can be represented as being in accord with the reigning Pope. What is the Protestant's answer? Mainly this: The Scriptures are interpreted from the shared experiences of the believing community, the Holy Spirit witnessing in each, and in each to each, of the truth of what is intended for us.

Great as are the changes which have taken place in the view of the universe from that held by Luther, Calvin or Knox, nevertheless in the great essential the modern Protestant recognizes the great truths which they expressed. To each seeker, as to them, God has made His will known in nature, in history and, most clearly of all, in the person of our Lord Jesus Christ. God speaks to man directly by His Holy Spirit, calling him out of sin and ignorance into the new life of the kingdom of God. This faith in God's power to speak directly to men today explains the central place which is still given to the Bible by Protestants. Thus the Bible to the Protestants is both witness and invitation, a witness to the great things God has done in the past, an invitation to share the greater experience He will make possible today and tomorrow—a redemption that shall not only include all men, but all parts of the life of man.

"Isn't the Bible still our best seller?" you ask. "Yes," I answer. The Bible is the best seller in all the world, selling at the rate of more than 6,000,000 copies per year. It is read every Sunday in a million churches and church schools, and in over 900 languages and dialects. But that is not enough. Someone has truly said that many of the Bibles given away should be inscribed: "From one who has not read it to another who will do likewise." It is not enough to get inside the Bible; we must get the Bible inside us. It is not enough to possess it; we need to be possessed by it—by its message.

Dr. Charles Clayton Morrison says:

Nowhere does the Bible claim to be an authority above Christ or upon which his authority depends. Its Old Testament looks forward to him. Its New Testament bears witness to his life, teaching, death and resurrection; in factual account, in poetic vision and in discursive interpretation. The Bible is not the source of our faith, or the ground of it, or the proof of it. Christ alone is the source, the ground and the proof of our faith. The Bible is the nourisher of our faith, of our devotion and of our understanding of Christ. It is auxiliary to the authority of Christ, not a substitute for it.[6]

There is no claim in the Bible or by the Protestants who read and study it that it is an authority above Christ. The claim is made that the Bible is the story of man's search for God. It is the story of the life of the early Hebrews and of prophecies made by some of them who foretold the coming of Christ. The New Testament relates the story of his life and work. Jesus revealed the Gospel of Good News about God, what He is, and the good news about man, what he may become through the redeeming love of God.

It is well for us to recall that the Reformers insisted that the Bible, the authentic Word of God, be open to all men, for they held that an honest faith was required to understand the Scriptures properly. Luther contended "the common man,

[6] Dr. Charles Clayton Morrison, *Can Protestantism Win America?* (New York, Harper & Brothers, 1948), p. 138. Reprinted by permission of the publishers.

the boy of nine, the miller's maid, with the Bible know more about divine truth than the Pope without the Bible."

It is well to heed the words of Ernest von Dobschutz, who wrote:

Whenever a single individual, layman or theologian, has been enabled to draw fresh and full out of the Bible and present to others what he has obtained, the inward life of Christendom has been raised to a higher level.[7]

The Bible is everybody's book, for it tells of the struggle of the human soul. William Lyon Phelps, former Professor at Yale University, declares: "You can learn more about human nature by reading the Bible than by living in New York City."[8]

The Bible is a collection of sixty-six books or letters. It is a veritable library in one volume. It is a masterpiece in literature and merits top rating in what De Quincey rightly called "The Literature of Power." The Reformers discovered the Bible as the source of power because of its testimony to Christ and therefore they acknowledged its authority.

A right understanding of the four cardinal principles of our faith will help us "render back our true account" to God. Christianity gives to mankind both hope and power. Because we have such hope and power we can stand up to life unafraid and unashamed. The Canadian poet, Archibald Lampman, with penetrating insight, wrote:

Not to be conquered by these headlong days,
But to stand free: to keep the mind at brood
On life's deep meaning, nature's attitude
Of loveliness, and time's mysterious ways:

---

[7] William G. Chanter, "Protestantism and the Bible," in *Protestantism, a Symposium* (Nashville, Tenn., The Methodist Church, 1944), p. 142.

[8] "The Bible in the Church," *Encyclopaedia of Religion and Ethics*, II, 150.

At every thought and deed to clear the haze
Out of our eyes, considering on this,
What man, what life, what love, what beauty is,
This is to live, and win the final praise.[9]

---

[9] Archibald Lampman, *Lyrics of Earth* (Toronto, The Musson Book Company, Ltd., 1925). Reprinted by permission of the publishers.

5

THE SOLE AUTHORITY

AN UNKNOWN author has written simply and effectively of Jesus, the "One Solitary Life" that has for more than nineteen hundred years challenged all thoughtful men by its spiritual insight and moral grandeur:

Here is a man who was born in an obscure village, the child of a peasant woman. He grew up in another obscure village. He worked in a carpenter shop until he was thirty, and then for three years he was an itinerant preacher. He never wrote a book. He never held an office.

He never owned a home. He never set foot in a big city. He never traveled two hundred miles from the place where he was born. He had no credentials but himself.

He had nothing to do with this world except the naked power of his divine manhood. While still a young man, the tide of popular opinion turned against him. His friends ran away. One of them denied him. He was turned over to his enemies. He went through the mockery of a trial. He was nailed upon a cross between two thieves.

His executioners gambled for the only piece of property he had on earth while he was dying—and that was his coat. When he was dead he was taken down and laid in a borrowed grave through the pity of a friend.

Nineteen wide centuries have come and gone, and today he is the centerpiece of the human race and the leader of progress. I am far within the mark when I say that all the armies that ever marched, and all the navies that ever were built, and all the parliaments that ever sat, and all the kings that ever reigned, put together, have not affected the life of man upon this earth as powerfully as that One Solitary Life.

To the true Protestant Reformers of all ages, Jesus has been "the sole authority" of Protestant faith and practice. What then, do we mean when we say, "I believe in Jesus"? It is a profound question which we reverently ask. No easy or superficial answer will suffice. Let us grant at once that it is difficult to write objectively about Jesus, for he has meant so much to us.

"The life of Jesus Christ cannot be written." This has long been a commonplace with historians and biographers.

And yet what life has been so often written? Not, indeed, with the precision and fulness of information the ideal biography demands, and yet more movingly and tellingly than any other person's history. For the story of Jesus and how he flashed like a meteor across the sky of his generation and this world cannot be told too often. Adequately, it can indeed never be written, but though all other life stories fade from the memory of men, it must never be forgotten, for its sheer influence on human thought, human relations and human destiny, and for its incomparable contribution to man's faith in good and goodness. But who is sufficient to do these things?[1]

A verse from the well-known hymn expresses our feeling:

> Jesus, Thou joy of loving hearts,
> Thou fount of life, Thou light of men,
> From the best bliss that earth imparts,
> We turn unfilled to Thee again.

When we say, "I believe in Jesus," we mean that he was the Jesus of history. He lived! He was a historical figure.

---

[1] Edgar J. Goodspeed, *A Life of Jesus* (New York, Harper & Brothers, 1950), p. 11. Reprinted by permission of the publishers.

Yet the question whether he was a man who was born, lived and died—one who walked the earth as a man of flesh and blood, not a phantom—a myth, or a God, has been a matter of real controversy for years. To answer the question, Was Jesus a human being? was the primary effort of the Christian leaders as they formulated statements of faith, notably the one called Apostles' Creed. This creed not only states, "I believe in God the Father Almighty, Maker of Heaven and Earth," but it goes on to affirm "and in Jesus Christ His only Son, our Lord; who was conceived by the Holy Spirit, born of the Virgin Mary, suffered under Pontius Pilate, was crucified, dead and buried."

To the Protestants, there are no barriers to asking questions. Critical questioning arises with earnestness about the Church, about the Bible, and primarily about the life, teaching, death and significance of Jesus. Nothing is too sacred to be investigated. Christ can stand investigation. "Christianity stands or falls, lives or dies with the personality of Jesus Christ." From the standpoint of organized Christianity, the personality of Jesus is central. We will never rightly reform the Church except as we rediscover him and renew our lives by taking him in earnest. We cannot propagate Christianity anywhere, unless we present Jesus Christ as teacher, Lord and Saviour.

Therefore, the documents which claim to narrate his life and work must be studied by the same methods that we employ in investigating other records of the past. That method is necessary in order to maintain the intellectual integrity of our faith. The Protestant puts no premium on consecrated ignorance or credulity. The true Protestant asks questions and seeks answers.

Days of confusion and trouble have driven many to consider earnestly the meaning of Jesus for the experience of men, to ask with a great urgency what help he has for us in this perplexing age in which we live. Two kinds of questions are raised: First, what did Jesus actually teach and do? Second, what meaning does Jesus have for us? The answer to the first question is found in the four Gospels, which are practically our only sources of knowledge about Jesus' life. A very few sayings, such as the one found in Acts 2:36-37:

Therefore let all the house of Israel know assuredly, that God hath made that same Jesus, whom ye have crucified, both Lord and Christ. Now, when they heard this, they were pricked in their heart, and said unto Peter and to the rest of the apostles, Men and brethren, what shall we do?

and those scarce references made to Jesus in the writings of the third and fourth centuries, have been cherished sources. For any extensive knowledge of what Jesus said and did, we are dependent ultimately on the four New Testament Gospels: Matthew, Mark, Luke and John.

It is usually held that Mark was written earliest, about A.D. 70, and presents Jesus as a man of action. Matthew and Luke, who used Mark as their source, were probably written between A.D. 70 and A.D. 100, in which Jesus was pre-eminently presented as a teacher. Since Matthew and Luke both contain considerably more than Mark, particularly of the teaching of Jesus, and are similar in material, it is assumed that they both depended on a second source now lost. This source has been generally described as "Q."

The fourth Gospel was written considerably later than the other three. According to its author's statement, it was written to fulfill the definite purpose as stated in John 20:30-31:

And many other signs truly did Jesus in the presence of his disciples, which are not written in this book: But these are written, that ye might believe that Jesus is Christ, the Son of God; and that believing ye might have life through his name.

Thus it is evident that this book was intended, not merely to chronicle the life of Jesus, but to reveal the meaning of John's personal religious experience. John's Gospel is in the nature of a devotional biography with the emphasis placed upon Jesus as the source of religious power for the believer.

We can never unify the Christian Church except around Jesus Christ, by making his spirit and purpose central in our lives. The records of Jesus' life, teaching, work and death are largely found in the New Testament. This has led some scholars in the past to deny that he was a historical figure because they contended the Gospels were unreliable historical records. The answer to this contention has been repeatedly given by the best scholars of the world and their conclusion is this: Jesus was a historical figure. The answer has been so conclusively given that he was a real person in history that no reliable scholar in recent years has raised the question. We may therefore affirm confidently that Jesus was a real historical figure and go on to consider his life and its meaning for us.

The foundation of all true religion is faith in God. This is an accepted fact. But that which has given to Christianity its distinctive quality is faith in Jesus Christ. We believe in God; and we believe also in Jesus, for he most perfectly revealed God to man. Not only does Jesus reveal God to man, but he reveals man to himself. This dual role of revelation as to God, what He is, and as to man, what he may become when he is reconciled to God through Christ, makes Jesus the sole authority for the Protestant.

It will be generally recognized that to speak of the meaning of Jesus Christ is to speak of what is most distinctive and most decisive in Christian life and faith. The Christian religion, in whatever form, finds its center, and, it might also be said, its circumference also, in Christ. It is Christ who both distinguishes and unites the Church.[2]

This able appraisal is made by that distinguished New Testament scholar, John Knox, Professor of Union Theological
Seminary, New York City, in his book *On the Meaning of
Christ.*

Jesus is our clearest revelation of the will of God for man.
For all Protestants, God's purpose and character have always
centered in Jesus Christ. The use of the term Jesus Christ
must be recognized as most important. The Jesus of history
and the Christ of faith are both required to make complete
the understanding of this life.

What does it mean to believe "in Jesus Christ, His Son,
our Lord?" It means, first of all, that we look to Jesus to see
what God is, and we find our hearts and minds agree with
his great saying, "He that hath seen me hath seen the Father."
The supreme person must be the best revelation of God's
innermost nature. For many who have come to appreciate,
through modern scientific study, the vastness of the facts and
forces in the world, the face of a friendly Father has seemed
to disappear. But when we catch sight of "the glory of God
in the face of Jesus Christ":

> That one Face, far from vanish, rather grows,
>   Or decomposes but to recompose,
> Becomes my universe that feels and knows![3]

Christ is also the interpreter of God's revelation, both in
history and in the Bible. The greatest thing the Bible gives

[2] John Knox, *On the Meaning of Christ* (New York, Charles Scribner's
Sons, 1947), p. 1. Reprinted by permission.

[3] From Robert Browning's "Epilogue: Dramatis Personae," in *Masterpieces
of Religious Verse* (New York, Harper & Brothers, 1948), p. 135. Reprinted
by permission.

us is Jesus himself. Without him, the Bible cannot be understood. Through him, its message is clear and authoritative. This means that the authority of everything in the Bible is to be tested by the mind, the will and the spirit of Christ.

The practical question we face is: "Who is this Jesus whom men call Christ, the Son of God?" Our first answer, as we have noted, is that he was a man. He lived a short life of some thirty-three years in the little land of Palestine. When he was about thirty years old, to the great astonishment of members of his family and his friends, he gave up his work as a carpenter and began to teach. He is now everywhere acknowledged as one of the greatest teachers of religion in all the world, if not the very greatest. He taught that faith in God leads to the transforming of life and to purposeful living.

Jesus Christ is our Lord and Saviour. Or to state the same idea in a different way: Jesus is God's great gift to *save* the world. We call Jesus Christ *Saviour*. A saviour does something for us, we are more than *saved* from something—we are saved *for* something, some great plan. He saved us by introducing us to God, His will and His purpose. "What is the chief end of man?" is the well-known question in the Westminster Confession of Faith. And the answer is: "To glorify God and enjoy Him forever." Christ is the true light of God for us, "reliable for truth and saving for life."

"Jesus was born in Bethlehem of Judea in the days of Herod the king"—that is the Jesus of history. "I live, yet not I, but Christ liveth in me"—that is the Christ of faith. The Jesus of history is necessary. But it is not enough to trace the outline of his life from his birth to his death. If our religion is to be vital, we must also believe in the Christ of Faith.

> Though Christ a thousand times
> In Bethlehem be born,

> If he's not born in thee
> Thy soul is still forlorn.[4]

We cannot keep Christ back in history—he is in us, deep
and abiding. To say with Paul, "I live, yet not I, but Christ
liveth in me," is not only good theology; it is a vital part of
Christian life experience.

In the following of Jesus, while doubts throng and answers
are delayed, decisions must be made. The question, after all,
is ours. It was a real question when Pilate asked it. It is a
real question now. We have Jesus on our hands.

> What think ye of Christ, friend? when all's
>   done and said,
> Like you this Christianity or not?
> It may be false, but will you wish it true?
> Has it your vote to be so if it can?[5]

Browning's question in "Bishop Blougram's Apology" is also
ours. My answer is that one man with an intelligent conviction is worth a thousand men with mere opinions, living ever
in the problem area of life, pooling their ignorance and refus-
ing to shoulder their responsibilities.

The recovery of the Christian message in its purity is the
greatest achievement of the Reformers. By recentering the
faith of the Christian fellowship in the sole lordship of Jesus
Christ over the Church and the world, the birth of Protestantism is assured. Before the profound mystery of the incarna-
tion—God manifested in the flesh, in a human life, divine
humility and grace—we shall forever stand wonderingly, in
adoring amazement. The extravagant love of God for all is

---

[4] From Angelus Silesius' "In Thine Own Heart" in *Masterpieces of Religious Verse*, p. 148. Reprinted by permission.

[5] From Robert Browning's "Bishop Blougram's Apology," in *The Complete
Poetic and Dramatic Works of Robert Browning* (Boston, Houghton Mifflin
Company, 1895). Reprinted by permission.

beyond the grasp of human comprehension. Only God could have thought of Christmas! All of our Christologies are but the feeble approximation of the great truth embodied in Jesus, the Christ.

It is not hard to get most of us to praise Jesus Christ. It is not too difficult to get some of us to study his life. But when we are asked to follow him—that is the acid test. Dean Inge had us all in mind when he said, "We are losing our Christianity because Christianity is a creed for heroes, while we are mainly harmless, good-natured little people, who want everybody to have a good time."

How can we follow Jesus? There are many answers. One I would stress: Christ should be a power, not a problem. Jesus should be a door which invites us in, not a wall that shuts out. Jesus Christ should be a help, not a hindrance to faith. Yet is this always the case?

Our times are serious. Life, deep down, always is serious. There is now, at last, little place for its lighter sides until the more serious sides have been attended to.

Everywhere men are searching for faith. They have to have some faith. They need a faith that they can live by and die by. They want no sham, no sentimentalities, no pious moonings. Neither do they want stony dogmas, but the bread of the living truth.[6]

This faith for living is found in Jesus Christ. With the author of Hebrews, we can say in truth, "We see not yet all things put under him [man]. *But we see Jesus.*"

Jesus was not blind to the evil in man, but there was something else he never lost sight of—the wonderful latent goodness in ordinary men and women. His standards were high, but he knew that the power of God is available to man, who is not left alone, an orphan in a mad, mad world. Jesus repeat-

---

[6] Nels S. Ferré, *Pillars of Faith* (New York, Harper & Brothers, 1948), p. 13. Reprinted by permission of the publishers.

edly emphasized the truth that if we would get into touch with God, we would find ourselves able "to rise on stepping stones of our dead selves" to higher and better things, and be enabled to live worthily and to live out life in some splendid conclusion.

He tested it out in his life, and found it true—that we may live victorious lives only by the grace of God. It is not enough for us to go back to the historical Jesus for a way of life. So many do that, and stop there. If Jesus' way of life is to become a reality for us, we, too, must learn to live by the help and grace of God, which Jesus revealed and made available to man. You and I may draw on divine resources. Does Christ's way seem too demanding, beyond our reach? Does it seem as if no one could attain unto it? Remember what Jesus told his disciples: "With man it is impossible, but with God all things are possible."

"God was in Christ, reconciling the world unto himself . . . We pray you in Christ's stead, be ye reconciled to God." So wrote Paul (Second Corinthians 5:19-20). It is at once the glory and doom of man to have been made for fellowship with God. It is his glory, for it opens up before him endless possibilities of spiritual achievement. It is his doom, because he can never wholly escape the down-drag of his nature and the compulsion of his destiny. Therefore he is a creature of tension. "Restless is our heart," said St. Augustine, "until it finds rest in thee."

Reconciliation with God is, therefore, the cardinal issue confronting the soul of man today. Reconciliation with God who made us and made us for Himself means also reconciliation within ourselves and between ourselves and others. In time, reconciliation is salvation. It is found in the redeemed and restored community who believe in and practice the Christian fellowship. It was not through obedience to the Jewish law, or to the authority of the Roman Catholic

Church, that the reconciliation of an estranged humanity was accomplished. "In Christ, God reconciled the world unto Himself." Paradoxically here is our freedom and our enslavement that sets us free.

The Gospel is not a book; it is a message. It is not good advice; it is good news; the good news about what God is and has done and is doing. Jesus called God "Abba" which means "Father." The word characterizes the distinctive thought of God whose just, seeking, forgiving love knows no end. Jesus is the unveiling of God in a human life; he is God in man.

Jesus defines God, but he does not confine Him [writes Dr. Henry Sloane Coffin], for God manifests Himself in myriad forms and comes to us along countless paths. Jesus is not the exclusive or exhaustive disclosure of the Father, but he is the distinctive revelation of his character and purpose.[7]

In view of all Jesus has done for mankind and all that he continues to be to those who trust him, we cannot express our conviction by saying less than that in him God has come among us in His fullness and given us His very self.

> Jesus, the very thought of thee
> With sweetness fills my breast;
> But sweeter far Thy face to see,
> And in Thy presence rest.
>
> O hope of every contrite heart,
> O joy of all the meek,
> To those who fall, how kind Thou art,
> How good to those who seek.[8]

---

[7] Dr. Henry Sloane Coffin, *Ventures in Belief* (New York, Charles Scribner's Sons, 1930), p. 54. Reprinted by permission of the publishers.

[8] Anonymous Latin hymn, eleventh century. Translated by E. Caswall in 1848.

Jesus, as his contemporaries saw him, cannot be thought of, therefore, in his stark historicity, as an uninterpreted person. His very first disciples began interpreting him, and so far as the four Gospels are concerned, this theological rendering of Jesus, which came to its climax in John, began in Mark. By various paths, these first followers came to him, wanting renewed faith, forgiveness of sin, healing of body and spirit, a leader to follow, a cause to serve, a hope to give them courage; and, finding these timeless needs supplied by Jesus, they began asking, Who is he? and answering in terms of the mental categories they had inherited. This, too, is a perennial process and still goes on. For the deep and abiding needs of man, in the twentieth century as in the first, call for a living, personal revelation and symbol of God, for pardon, power, faith in divine purpose and courage in serving it, for inward peace, a cause worth ultimate self-sacrifice and for hope here and hereafter.[9]

No wonder that Protestant Christians find in Jesus their sole authority, their "Lord and Master." The Gospel is the good news of God's plan and purpose revealed in Christ for man's redemption. Jesus Christ is the human side of God. Jesus is the idea made flesh. "In the beginning was the Word," i.e., the idea, "and the Word was made flesh." That is the Gospel which the Reformers rediscovered in the sixteenth century. "I am a Protestant," and therefore, I must rediscover for myself the Gospel of Jesus and bring it to bear on my life and on my needy day and generation. For Jesus Christ is the sole authority of the Protestant Christian. To him alone belongs our glad loyalty, our intelligent devotion and our unceasing love.

> O dearly, dearly hath he loved
> And we must love him too;
> And trust in his redeeming love
> And try his work to do.

---

[9] Harry Emerson Fosdick, *The Man From Nazareth* (New York, Harper and Brothers, 1949), pp. 247-248. Reprinted by permission of the publishers.

6

WHY BELIEF IS IMPORTANT

THERE are those who contend that it is not what you believe that matters; it is what you do that is important. Nay! What you do depends on what you believe. What you believe determines, in large measure, what you are and what you will do. One's life is thought-built. The verse in Proverbs, "As he thinketh in his heart, so is he," is a demonstrated truth. It is impossible to separate what a man thinks and believes from what he is. Beliefs determine the nature of one's character and one's life.

Therefore, one's belief in the essential Christian doctrines is most important. The doctrines deal with topics of life— its meaning and purpose, its source and destiny. It is encouraging to note that in recent years there has been an awakened interest in belief. There is a growing acknowledgment of the truth that everyone has to believe in something, in Someone higher than himself, or else he is like "an infant crying in the night whose only language is a cry."

The question "How can one believe?" is not so important; the real question is "What should one believe?" Believing means choosing. More, it means living by one's choice. For what one chooses one becomes. Belief is to learn the truth about God and one's self. Belief in God and belief in man are inseparable.

The freedom to believe is God's great gift to man. With it goes man's freedom to doubt. Honest doubt is right. Doubt is an integral part of all intelligent thinking. A concerned person deserves more than satire when he voices his doubts. He must, however, learn to doubt his doubts. G. K. Chesterton once said that the men who finally brought him to orthodoxy were the atheists. As he said, "They sowed in my mind my first wild doubts of doubt." Honest doubt is an aid to vital Christian faith. "There is more truth in honest doubt than in half the creeds." Long before Dostoevski, Jesus saw this truth: "The secret of man's being is not only to live, but to have something to live for." There is need today for knowing what one believes for clear and clean-cut thinking, so that one may put into faith a positive intellectual content. Otherwise, one comes to a dead-end road and life ends in futility.

It is significant that when the fundamental law of religion, which was stated in the Old Testament, "Thou shalt love the Lord, Thy God, with all thine heart and with all thy soul and with all thy might," emerges in the New Testament, it is with the last phrase changed, "with all thy mind." There may be forms of pseudo religion which demand that one cease thinking when he enters the Church, but true Protestant Christianity calls us to serve God and man thoughtfully.

God does not bless consecrated ignorance or any kind of ignorance. It is, therefore, a vital matter for the Christian of today to know what he believes, and then to live by that faith. He, as a Protestant, holds it to be the right of every individual to think and form judgments for himself. Nowhere in the world is there any external authority which can dictate to the individual Protestant Christian precisely what he shall or shall not believe. Everyone must do his own thinking in the sight of God, and give account for the way he has used that privilege or duty. No man has the right to say to one, "You believe this or that, or you be damned."

The greatest sin which can be committed against man is to

say to him: "You shall not think!" To think for one's self about the great Christian beliefs will enable one to grow in Christian stature. One should strive to be different from other people who are indifferent. If one believes in the great realities of the Christian faith, and another does not, there should be a marked difference between them. If one believes and is different, perhaps those who do not believe will not be indifferent to great Christian truths.

All mankind, like Gaul, is divided into three parts. First, there are those who are skeptical. Second, there are the great believers, those who are ever questing for the highest and the best—even for God. They are sensitive to His presence and purpose. Between these two groups, the unbelievers and the believers, there is the largest group, to which most people belong, those who want to believe, need to believe, but are having poor success in achieving a satisfying belief. Their cry is: "Lord I believe, help thou my unbelief."

People are born to believe. They cannot live on questionings. For a man to say in honesty, "I do not believe that dogma," may be a virtue, provided he can add with radiant mind, "Yet I do believe this . . ." But without some positive avowal his negations become only darkness, for belief is as native as breathing. People cannot live on "facts." Facts are not faith.[1]

This is an age of belief, not unbelief, but one is too often content in make-believes. One must believe in something, something to hold to, something to give meaning and purpose to life; aye, one must believe in Someone. Very often one believes in the wrong thing and in the wrong person. Because of this fact, it is necessary to examine the creed and theology

---

[1] George A. Buttrick, *So We Believe, So We Pray* (New York and Nashville, Abingdon-Cokesbury Press, 1951), pp. 17-18. Reprinted by permission of the publishers.

for one's self. A creed is a statement of what a man or group of men believes and acts on. One must have a theology, for theology deals with a man's equilateral relationship with God and his fellow men. It is the understanding of what God is, and what man can become under His creative touch.

Too often the Protestant has taken his belief for granted; therefore he has not examined it, either to question or affirm. The pious acceptance of faith in general without examination often leads to indifference, if not to a partial rejection of faith. This uncritical attitude develops in many a dogmatic adherence to a set of beliefs which is difficult either to deny or affirm successfully. One must examine his beliefs, for it is by beliefs that life is lived. It was the thoughtlessness of many which led Samuel Butler to remark that the Christian people of his time would be "shocked to hear the Christian faith doubted, and equally surprised to see it practiced."

That all life is based on beliefs of some kind is the main thought of the book entitled *Ideas Have Legs*. Belief comes from ideas that have been examined by the mind and tested and retested in living. There was never a truer word than that of Carlyle when he said that the religious belief of a man is the chief fact concerning him. By religious belief he meant, as he went on to explain, not the creed to which a man subscribes or otherwise gives his assent; not that necessarily, often not that at all—since we see men of all degrees of worth and worthlessness signing all manner of creeds. By religious belief Carlyle meant that which a man believes practically, lays to his heart often enough without asserting it to himself, acts on, and knows concerning this mysterious universe and his duty and destiny in it. This in all cases is the primary thing in him, and creatively determines all the rest; this is his religion. If you know this about a man, you know what he is and what he will do and what he may become.

We believe in man. We believe in men not merely as production units, but as the children of God. We believe that the purpose of our society is not primarily to assure the "safety of the State" but to safeguard human dignity and the freedom of the individual. As a people we have built upon a faith in the spirit of man. We conceive that the development and happiness of the individual is the purpose and goal of American life. We are not ready to "trade in" this luminous concept of a people's purpose for the notion that the America of the Bill of Rights, of Walt Whitman and Justice Holmes and Abraham Lincoln, is simply a highly productive economic system.[2]

What are the beliefs of Protestant Christians? There are certain cardinal beliefs which are common to all denominations: the just goodness of God, the redemptive power of Christ, the worth of the individual as a child of God, the value of the Church as a group of people having fellowship with one another and with God through Christ and learning how to live redemptively and triumphantly. Aye, it is what he believes that really determines the nature of the man and what shall be the nature of his existence as a member of society.

To Luther faith was the personal act of the believer. "If you believe, you have" was the ruling principle which he constantly reiterated. It was a gift of God, not obtained by penance or works for merit. Luther's position regarding salvation was "not by charity, not by works, but by faith alone." Faith is not easily or rationally understood; it is a trust. "For this is the nature of faith, that it dares to trust in God's grace," a free commitment and joyful, daring adventure, based upon the extravagant goodness of God.

After all, faith is not belief in spite of evidence, but life in scorn of consequence—a courageous trust in the great purpose

---

[2] David E. Lilienthal, *This I Do Believe* (New York, Harper & Brothers, 1949), p. 18. Reprinted by permission of the publishers.

of all things and pressing forward to finish the work which is in sight, whatever the price may be.

Thus in vivid and refreshing terms, Kirsopp Lake states his affirmation.

Luther contended that faith must be a personal experience—a Christian has faith by virtue of a personal deed and decision in order to make it valid. You yourself must decide. This naturally resulted in a tragic tension. On the one hand, faith was the gift of God who acts upon man from without; on the other hand, it was a personal decision and commitment from within. This led to the agonizing experience which dominated much of Luther's life and the lives of men like him throughout history. These men had "dark hours of the soul"; they saw God and yet they had to live on earth as a part of Caesar's household. As Josiah Royce declared: "Faith is the discovery of a Reality that enables a man to face anything that happens to him in the universe."

The one who does not believe that the universe is friendly, or that there is in it somewhere a force which makes for righteousness, can never rise to the level of one who casts anchor in the living Son of God. Such a faith is both a venture and a commitment. It marks the difference between darkness and light, between death and life. Listen to one who proclaims the way into that zone of absolute certainty. "He that believeth on the Son of God hath the witness in him." John Oxenham sings with a clear, strong voice:

> "Not what, but *Whom,* I do believe,
>   That, in my darkest hour of need,
>   Hath comfort that no mortal creed
>   To mortal man may give;—
>   Not what, but *Whom!*
>   For Christ is more than all the creeds,
>   And His full life of gentle deeds
>   Shall all the creeds outlive.

"Not what I do believe, but *Whom!*
Who walks beside me in the gloom?
Who shares the burden wearisome?
Who all the dim way doth illume,
And bids me look beyond the tomb
The larger life to live?—
Not what I do believe,
But *Whom!*
Not what
But *Whom!*"[3]

According to Professor C. A. Scott, formerly of Union Theological Seminary, "The burden of the Lord's teaching was, Have faith in God." The Roman Catholic Church teaches: "Have faith in the priest, and accept what he says without question." There is a wide difference between the Protestants and the Roman Catholics in their ideas of worship, the sacraments, the clergy and the Church. As the Reformers came to see, the conception of the Protestant Church goes back to the spirit of the New Testament Church, which arose out of the fact that those who believed in God, as revealed in Jesus Christ, were bound to one another by His love into a fellowship of believers and declared, "I know whom I have believed."

Is "faith" the same as "belief?" Often the words are used interchangeably, although more often there is a difference in connotation. We tend to speak of faith when we are designating the less sure beliefs. We believe our eyes, and we believe the proposition that twice two are four, but we have faith in America, or in the ultimate triumph of good over evil. There is, of course, a borderline of discourse where we can use either term. "I believe in the United Nations" means much the same as "I have faith in the United Nations."

"Faith" also seems to carry a warmer glow of affection

---

[3] John Oxenham, "Credo" in *Masterpieces of Religious Verse,* p. 368. Reprinted by permission.

than does bare "belief." It suggests that, though the risk may be greater, still the commitment is stronger and the outcome of the wager more precious. Most people, when asked, say they believe in God. But in many of these cases, the reply seems perfunctory, and one suspects that the religious sentiment behind the statement is rudimentary. But when an individual says, "I have faith in God," it seems almost certain that the religious sentiment holds a prominent place in his personality structure.[4]

Jesus believed in institutions as a means, not an end, but he was no institutionalist in the sense of one who stresses the primacy of institutions. For Jesus, the two essentials in religion were revelation and faith—"the divine disclosure and the human response," as Bruner stated it. Beside faith, all other human energies or institutions or observances are secondary! So the Protestant Reformation brought to the fore the conviction that the Church, with its worship and sacraments, is secondary, existing only to serve faith.

Dr. Joseph Haroutunian, in his recent book *Lust for Power*, says:

It is most disturbing to realize that our culture cannot endure without faith whose authentic language in Christendom is the Apostles' Creed. How then can there be hope for "this faithless generation?" There is too much infatuation with machines and goods, too much misunderstanding of the Christian faith within the churches, as well as outside them; too much unacknowledged despair and too little conviction of guilt; too much power, tempting men and nations to lord it one over another. Besides, religion itself is much too uncritical and uncreative. If our future depends upon our faith, our case appears hopeless. Still, we do not know our future as settled. The Christian faith has deep roots in our history and culture. We may think as atheists and feel as esthetes, but we

---

[4] Gordon W. Allport, *The Individual and His Religion* (New York, The Macmillan Company, 1950), p. 123. Reprinted by permission of the publishers.

do not and cannot exist without faith. We still care about justice, freedom, order, self-respect, common weal, which are fruits of faith. There are many among us who hate the misuse of men and the lording of one man over another. There are humble men and women everywhere who have not lost their humanity and might "in a pinch" decide to live as human beings rather than die as fiends. And so long as they exist, they exist ambiguously; they exist by faith, and they may act wisely. In a society formed by the Christian faith, there are hidden as well as visible powers making for wisdom. The boundless energy which the Christian faith has released in the world is not spent. To an alarming extent it has become lustful, and is driving us toward ruin. But still, signs of its beneficent working are everywhere, and it is in truth possible that it will become effective toward a new life of wisdom and justice among us.[5]

Move up and down the Gospels and see how often Jesus presses home the importance of belief. "Ye believe in God, believe also in me." "Ye have seen, and in seeing did not believe. Blessed are they that have not seen and yet have believed." Our beliefs lend us a truly amazing power. It is therefore well to remember Disraeli's advice: "Nurture your minds with great thoughts, for to believe in the heroic makes heroes."

Christian living has always been rooted in certain profound convictions about God and about man and about the world in which we live. While, as we have noted, it is very important to believe—merely to believe is not enough—it is far more important what we believe. For the life of mankind is being destroyed today, not because man has no beliefs, but because of man's deep belief in and loyalty to false and self-destroying ends. That is the terrible thing about Communism and war.

---

[5] Joseph Haroutunian, *Lust for Power* (New York, Charles Scribner's Sons, 1949), pp. 171-172. Reprinted by permission of the publishers.

In 1930 the editors of *Fortune Magazine* declared:

As laymen dedicated to the practice of Christianity we can merely record our certainty that in order for humanity to progress, it must believe; it must have faith in certain absolute spiritual values, or at least have faith that absolute spiritual values exist. . . . Without spiritual leadership the maladjustments of our politico-economic system must inevitably increase; unemployment, lack of opportunity, maldistribution of wealth and lack of confidence will symptomize a long retreat; collectivism will grow; and what remains to us of the golden age, when we were able to believe, will be consumed in revolutions and wars. . . .[6]

"It is the task of the Church to point the way out," continue the editors of *Fortune Magazine,* as reported in the *Christian Century.*

We are asked to turn to the Church for our enlightenment, but when we do so, we find that the voice of the Church is not inspired. The voice of the Church today, we find, is the echo of our own voices. And the result of this experience, already manifest, is disillusionment.

It took years to accumulate the ecclesiastical pomp, the high ritual, incense, candles, the Mass, the hierarchy and the seven sacraments, which became part and parcel of the Roman Catholic Church. While the great religious principles set forth in the New Testament were to a large measure obscured and lost during the Middle Ages, these principles were rediscovered and embraced by the Protestant Reformation, and it is equally important for Protestants today to rediscover and embrace them anew. There are many, but those four basic principles which we have reviewed are always to be considered and understood, if one is to know why one is a Protestant.

---

[6] *Fortune Magazine.*

One has a defective Christian experience if one does not believe, or at least wish to believe definitely in God our Father, and in Christ our Lord, and in man's relationship and responsibility to God through Christ. To believe in great realities, lying deep at the heart of the life of the world, is to live unshaken in a shaken world. What would it make of your life and mine, and of the life of the world, if we really believed that the maker and the sustainer of our life is our Father, God? We need to record our answer to this question.

Luther recorded his memorable answer. After pondering over the passage "By grace are ye saved, through faith; and that not of yourselves: it is the gift of God," and similar passages, he came to the conviction that faith is that act by which he commits himself in absolute dependence and child-like confidence on the grace and love of God as revealed in Jesus Christ. He thus recorded his convictions:

There are two kinds of believing: first, a believing about God which means that I believe what is said of God is true. This is rather a form of knowledge than a faith. Men possessing it can say, repeating what others have said: I believe that there is a God. I believe that Christ was born, died, rose again for me. But what the real faith is, and how powerful a thing it is, of this they know nothing. There is, secondly, a believing in God which means that I put my trust in Him, give myself up to thinking that I can have dealings with Him, and believe without any doubt that He will be and do to me according to the things said of Him. Such faith which throws itself upon God, whether in life or in death, alone makes a man a Christian.

It is of paramount importance for men and women really to believe that the need of this fearful day goes far deeper than any matter of special doctrine or treatise. It was Nietzche who said that the ideal man would be a Caesar with the soul of Christ. It is an impossible combination, for if Caesar

had the soul of Christ he would not be Caesar. He would be
restrained by the thought that humility and service are the
marks that Christ puts on power when it is mastered by his
spirit. To believe that and try to live it out is what it means to
build on Christ as the foundation. Men need to believe in
God—"Religion is betting your life there is a God"—a Christ-
like God. The questions we face in these dark days are real
and earnest. Back of the phenomena of life, is there a God
that can, in any real sense be called friendly, parental, just
and loving? Is man a cog in a machine, or a child in a home?
Someone has well said that the deepest and most significant
of all questions is this: "Is the universe friendly?" Put in a
different way, it is to ask, "Does God care?" These questions
require adequate, honest and positive answers.

Thoughtful men are seeking honest answers. Clarence B.
Randall, President of the Inland Steel Company, in an address
given on September 19, 1950, to the Comptrollers' Institute
of America, said:

Obviously, for those of us in this room, who are a selected
group, who possess, whether we know it or whether we want
it, a high degree of leadership, it is incumbent upon us to
make up our minds as to what we believe, why we believe it
and to do something about it.

Just as we reject in economics the concept of a dictator, so
in the realm of social philosophy, we must reject the concept
that America shall be oriented by the few. We believe that
the wisdom of the many is greater than the wisdom of the
few. And to guide America we need an awakened, aroused
and intelligent public opinion. Our people have gone lazy
intellectually. Our forebears lived in an atmosphere of vigorous debate on public questions. Men walked long, weary
miles to hear Lincoln debate Douglas—they won't walk
across the room to turn on the radio to hear a debate today.
They walk across the room to change the program if one
happens to be on in their presence.

We take our views from television and the radio and the

commentators and the comics. We haven't the intellectual honesty and the intellectual vitality to think things out. America needs to think—and, having thought, America needs to act. It is the job of every thoughtful industrial leader in this country to set an example by establishing in his own mind a thoughtful social philosophy and then to do something about it.

Thank you, Mr. Randall. Enlarge this statement to include the world and we have a criterion for Christian action.

If you and I would live all the time as men and women who genuinely and fully believe in "God, the Father Almighty, Maker of Heaven and Earth" and in "Jesus Christ, His only Son, our Lord," what sort of lives would we live? We know they would be lives of triumphant usefulness, full of poise, power and peace. Just a faith believed and lived would make a difference to which the world would not be indifferent. Then, with Paul, we could say:

For I am persuaded, that neither death, nor life, nor angels, nor principalities, nor powers, nor things present, nor things to come, nor height, nor depth, nor any other creature, shall be able to separate us from the love of God, which is in Christ Jesus, our Lord.

According to Glover, the historian, the early Christians "outthought the pagan world and hence outlived" it. They were the saints in Caesar's household.

A boy and his father were in a church. The father used the word *saint* in describing the figures in the windows. Turning to the boy, he said, "You do not know what saint means, do you?"

The boy replied, "Oh yes, they are the ones whom the light shines through."

So must we, who call ourselves Christians, if we are to

bring order out of chaos, peace out of conflict, and good out of tragic circumstances, have great beliefs and affirm:

I believe in God, Father Almighty, Maker of Heaven and Earth.

I believe in Jesus Christ, His only Son, our Lord, and his way of life.

I believe in man as a child of God and an inheritor of the promise of life abundant and eternal.

I believe in the Cross of Christ as the central point of history.

I believe in the resurrection as a vindication of the way of the Cross.

It is necessary that these beliefs become deeply rooted in the mind and will and life, and finely expressed in the living of everyone who truly says, "I am a Protestant."

7

THE WORLD IS TOO STRONG FOR A DIVIDED CHURCH

BISHOP BRENT, at one of the early international Church conferences, said: "The world is too strong for a divided Church." So it has been and is, and ever more shall be, unless the Church unites its strength—"in unity there is strength." The attempts by the Protestant churches to gain unity are worthy of our careful attention and evaluation. The world's decreasing size, resulting from man's technological developments, and the growing sense of human solidarity have broadened the horizons of race, nation and creed. An impetus toward church federations and church unions is derived from the practical necessity to achieve order and efficiency in a world where tolerance and co-operation must be substituted for rivalry and competition. Disillusionment with the fragmentary nature of historical processes, resulting in surrender to secularism, has awakened a new regard for spiritual power; and with the wide-flung frontiers of our day, the Protestant Church is impelled to rethink its mission in universal terms. Conditioned by the environment in which it exists, the Church is being challenged to place new confidence in its spiritual calling and to oppose vigorously and positively the world-wide secularism which threatens to engulf it.

The last twenty-five years have increasingly presented us with new signs of reunion and unity in the Protestant fellowship. In defiance of ancient tradition the new spirit has given birth to the younger churches in the foreign mission fields: to the united churches in India, Japan, China and Canada, and to various types of federated and organic church unions. The same spirit has sought new orientations in the world-wide discussion of "Faith and Order" and "Life and Work," and at the subsequent conferences in Stockholm and Amsterdam where the unity of the Spirit in the Body of Christ was variously reaffirmed. This quest for unity has given rise to a new vision of the one Universal Protestant Church. In this new atmosphere the Christian churches of the world seem ready, as never before, to take seriously the prayer of the Lord, "that they all may be one."

Much as we admire the motive and objective of this movement the methods must be carefully examined. We shall soon discover how difficult it is for denominations to unite at a level beyond federative unions, if particular historical legacies continue to embody the essential beliefs which must be taught, learned and held as the true doctrine once delivered by the saints. Where the impetus for the federation of churches and even for their union is inspired by practical expediency, or by the demand for more efficient and effective over-all administration, or by the romantic desire for a common Protestant front, or by the mere quest for power on the part of certain denominational leaders, the federation and unions fall short of the New Testament ideal.

THE LOCAL CHURCH

A strong, effective local Church with able leadership is required by the Protestant Church if it is to expand and spread its influence throughout the world. We can learn a very important lesson from the Roman Catholic Church in this regard. It has one Church, well equipped and well staffed, serving a given area or parish, frequently in contrast to many weak, competing Protestant churches in the same area. Nothing is so weak as a weak church. The local Church must take to itself the words of Jesus: "For whosoever will save his life shall lose it: but whosoever shall lose his life for my sake, the same shall save it." We must have strength at the grass roots—in the local Church. Gilbert K. Chesterton once made this wise observation: "Nothing is real until it is local."

THE COMMUNITY CHURCH

The Community Church is perhaps the most representative and distinctive feature of American Protestantism. It is interdenominational, drawing its members and ministers from many diverse communions. It is a separate, independent, autonomous congregation, self-supporting and democratic in its government. It has a real concern for the needs of the community.

The establishment of some 2,500 community churches in the last few years is an indication that many laymen have revolted against the folly of competing denominations, and that there has often been a lack of statesmanship on the part of denominational leaders. Local churches have wished to include all Protestants of the community in one fellowship. While there is much in favor of this movement, there are some arguments against it. These community churches have been "orphan churches" with no inclusive Protestant Church to give them a world-wide vision and a sense of "belonging." This situation has led to the forming of what in fact is another denomination. Some community churches have an affiliation with one of the already existing denominations. The Congregational-Christian churches have been singularly interesting and successful experiments.

The success of the relationship depends to a great extent on the minister of the local church. If he possesses a spirit of concern for the world-wide work of the Church, he can lead his people from being a smug country-club type of church to some sense of its privilege and responsibility in the larger fellowship of Christians. Too often the question of channeling benevolence money is the point of friction and the stumbling block to a real sense of "belonging" in one fellowship. The community churches may well be the forerunners of an all-inclusive Protestant Church, truly ecumenical in character. God, hasten the day!

Christians of various denominations cannot worship and work together in one community without discovering that the denominational differences are insignificant. Many of the issues which have made for division are obsolete and have lost their meaning to most intelligent Americans. In Europe Protestantism naturally developed national churches, but in America, where the people lived together in a common social environment, a "consciousness of kind" came to have more significance than denominational rivalries. They felt at home in any of the churches because the members of the various churches—Presbyterian, Episcopalian, Congregational, Reformed, Baptist and Methodist—were in general the same type of people, leading the same sort of life. This led naturally and inevitably to the establishment of a community church which included all people and denominations.

One of the significant churches in American Protestantism is Riverside Church in New York City. Although it is Baptist in tradition and has had as ministers Dr. Harry Emerson Fosdick and Dr. Robert J. McCracken, both Baptists, Riverside recruits its members from every sect and church and is largely supported by those who are opposed to denominational differences. Here is a symbol of American Protestantism looking for adequate expression. Other churches are also showing what can be done in the community field, notably the Community Church of Columbus, Ohio, and the Bryn Mawr Community Church of Chicago. The Bryn Mawr Church, of which I am the minister, has 42 different denominations in its fellowship. Each week about 5,000 people of all ages make use of the varied educational and religious programs available in its community house and sanctuary. During the last eight years over 2,300 people have been received into its membership. This church has 12 full-time and 16 part-time people as members of its paid staff.

THE FEDERATED CHURCH

Further evidence of the growing spirit of unity is found in the numerous mergers of existing local churches of different denominations into federated churches, preserving connections with denominational origins. Such mergers are usually motivated by laymen. The combinations have been helpful in many localities, especially as they represent the desire to minimize differences and emphasize common aims and purposes. The chief drawback is that the members lack the consciousness of definite "belonging," for now two denominations have a claim upon them rather than one. Here again, too often, ambitious and petty denominational leaders are the main cause of discontent and friction. Denominational zeal violates the eternal values to be preserved and comprises the cause of spiritual unity.

Is Protestantism permanently condemned to the fate which now holds it in the bondage of sectarian intolerance? Is there any hope that its leaders—the clergy, the large church secretariat, the bishops, the theologians, the editors of denominational papers will free themselves from the narrow limitations of a denominational mentality? There are evidences of hope that this may be accomplished in spite of those few smug denominationalists in the Protestant ranks who are as aloof as the Catholics from their other brethren in Christ.

UNION OF DENOMINATIONS

In the last few years "the scandal of the Protestant Church" in an increasing number of competing denominations has ceased. In fact the number has been markedly reduced by mergers. This process has been going on for some time but definite results have only quite recently been achieved.

Since 1906 fourteen such mergers have taken place. Others are now in process of negotiation. These mergers may be conceived as way stations on the road to an ecumenical Protestantism. They represent, negatively, a loosening of sectarian bonds which inevitably accompanies a sincere response to the ecumenical spirit, and they represent, positively, the longing of Christian people for a church more worthy of their allegiance than the sectarian fragment of the church whose weakness and irrelevance are increasingly apparent.[1]

This is the cogent judgment of Dr. Charles Clayton Morrison.

Dr. Morrison concludes his chapter entitled "Ecumenical Protestantism" with this statement:

In this general movement for the merger of denominations, what is now needed is the demonstration of the ecumenical principle by the merger of certain denominations whose sectarian features and traditions are unlike. This would constitute an unambiguous advance toward the ecumenical goal, because it would provide an example and a pattern for a similar union of multiple "churches" on a larger scale. For this reason, the negotiations between "churches" representing separate ecclesiastical traditions, such as the Congregational

---

[1] Dr. Charles Clayton Morrison, *Can Protestantism Win America?* (New York, Harper & Brothers, 1948), p. 162. Reprinted by permission of the publishers.

Christian with the Evangelical and Reformed, on the one hand, and the Episcopal with the Presbyterian, on the other, both now under way, carry great promise and are being watched with prayerful hope.[2]

In 1951, only three short years after Dr. Morrison's book was published, it is discouraging to report that the merger of the Congregational Christian with the Evangelical and Reformed has met with legal difficulties, and that the merger of the Episcopal with the Presbyterian is dormant.

Two plans for the union of denominations must be considered: one, the Federal Union Plan; second, a Plan of Union for a United Church.

THE FEDERAL UNION

This plan has as its chief advocate E. Stanley Jones, the internationally known and highly respected missionary, author and Christian statesman. What is the Federal Union Plan? In a nutshell, according to E. Stanley Jones, it is as follows:

1. The plan for federal union of the Churches goes beyond co-operation, as in councils of churches and federations, where sovereign denominations federate to do certain things together. It is union, organic union with a federal structure. The churches would come together on the same basis on which the colonies came together—union at the center with local self-government.

2. Federal union would result in one united church, the "Church of Christ in America" or the "United Church of America."

3. Under the one united church, there would be branches. The former separate, sovereign denominations would be branches of the one church—the Lutheran Branch of the

2 *Ibid.*, p. 163.

Church of Christ in America, the Baptist Branch, the Episcopal Branch, the African Methodist Episcopal Branch, the Nazarene Branch.

4. The total structure of the United Church would be: (a) the City Assembly of the Church of Christ in America; (b) the County Assembly; (c) the State Assembly; (d) the General or National Assembly; (e) the World Assembly.

5. Within the branches there would be local self-government, comparable to states' rights in our federal political union. If any branch now has, for example, bishops or adult baptism by immersion, it could keep those or any other distinguishing characteristics, but would not make acceptance of them by others the price of union.

6. Between branches there would probably be 90 per cent willing to have interchange of members and ministers and intercommunion. The other 10 per cent would be left to time and the spirit of God. (Rhode Island and North Carolina did not sign the Constitution at first.) However, any branch could make any condition, or no condition, for acceptance of members into its branch.

7. If any two or more branches should desire to merge or amalgamate they could do so under federal union. There would be that many fewer branches in the union. Union by amalgamation could go as far as it could go.

8. All property now held by the branches would continue to be held by the branches. Only property created by and for the union would be held by the union. There would thus be little or no difficulty over property under federal union.

9. The doctrinal basis could be the confession that Jesus is "the Christ, the Son of the Living God," for on the rock of that confession Jesus said he would build his church. Any branch that would make that confession would be considered "on the Rock."

10. The union would be not a union of uniformity but a union of diversity. Each branch would be invited to bring in its distinctive emphasis without compromise. For the union would be a union not of compromise but of comprehension.

11. The churches can come together on the same basis as the thirteen colonies came together. In both cases it would be a union of the people. In the case of the colonies they said:

"We the people . . . do hereby ordain and establish this Constitution." The federal government of the United States has
relationships primarily not with states but with the people
of the states. The people hold the sovereignty. But they
delegate some sovereignty to the states as a convenient unit
for representation, and then they delegate the final sovereignty
to the union.

The federal union of the churches would be a union of the
people of the churches. The people hold the sovereignty under
God. They delegate part of that sovereignty to the branch as
a convenient unit of representation and administration, and
the final sovereignty to the union. But the sovereignty, we
repeat, rests with the people under God.

12. In joining a local church, the candidate would declare
his loyalty to the branch and also to the union, thus holding
a dual loyalty, just as a citizen of the United States holds a
dual loyalty, to the state and to the nation.

13. Federal union puts together in a living blend the desire
for union with the whole and the desire for local self-government. It is based on human nature and the divine plan: "One
body . . . many members."

From the above we would deduce that federal union is
organic union because (1) it is based on the organic fact that
those who belong to Christ automatically belong to one another. Federal union basically declares that the union is not
around a minute sameness of doctrine, or sameness of church
government, or sameness of ordination ceremony; it is based
on a common loyalty to Christ. It says that there can be and
should be great diversity in these things if there is a common
loyalty to Christ. So federal union is organic union because it
is based on an organic relationship with Christ and not merely
on a mechanical contrivance in organization.

There are those who believe that the plan of the federal
union is "expressive of timidity rather than boldness" and
that a large section of Protestantism is now ready to go much
farther. They contend that the schemes of federal union do

not deal drastically enough with the 256 denominational systems; that the maintenance of the denominational machinery is too burdensome and costly; and that co-operation is not enough, although they realize that successful co-operation often leads to unity. They contend that only a united church makes sense to a laity which is thoroughly dissatisfied, if not disgusted, by our Protestant disunity.

A PLAN FOR UNION

The representatives of eight denominations met in a conference at Greenwich, Connecticut, late in 1949, and passed a resolution stating that it was their purpose to form an "organic union" of the Protestant churches. They appointed a continuing committee of the organization called the Conference on Church Union, and instructed that committee to study federal union and other plans, and to report at Cincinnati, Ohio, in December 1950.

At the meeting in Cincinnati, this committee made its report, and at the close of a fruitful session, a revised report was adopted which was to be sent to all churches. The report is as follows:

TO THE CHURCHES OF CHRIST OF THE UNITED STATES OF AMERICA: GREETINGS IN THE NAME OF OUR LORD JESUS CHRIST, THE HEAD OF THE CHURCH, WHOSE BODY THE CHURCH IS:

I. *The Divine Imperative*

We, the Conference on Church Union, consisting of officially appointed representatives of our several churches, gratefully recognize the initiative and guidance of God in the movement among all Christian people for a united church. The call for unity is a divine imperative and we believe that

union is an indispensable means to that end. We have long
known that in matters of faith we are already one. We now
rejoice in the discovery that the practical operations of our
several polities are strikingly similar.

Over many years there has been a steady growth of fra-
ternal fellowship, mutual cooperation, and the spirit of unity
among us. This has prompted us earnestly and prayerfully to
inquire what may be the next step in the development of our
responsibility for one another. Our common faith in Jesus
Christ as Lord and Savior makes us one body in him, and in
penitence for our present unhappy separation from one another, we believe that our Master now calls us to transcend
those barriers which divide us into various and often competing denominations and churches.

Today, Christians confront a world situation which demands that the churches shall make common cause. In our
own and many other sections of the world, secularism, atheism
and religious indifferentism are strongly entrenched and militant. These evil forces stand sharply over against the Christian church with its eternal gospel of redemption. They
cannot be effectively resisted and overcome by separate
churches, but only by the personal and corporate witness and
the concerted action of Christians united. In the broad perspective of the world scene, and in view of our great common
convictions and concerns, our denominational differences appear inconsequential.

In our meetings together, in prayer and prolonged delibera-
tion, we have reached a common conviction that the time has
now come when all the churches must take with profound
seriousness both the divine and the practical mandate for a
united church. We look forward in faith and hope to a more
comprehensive union than that envisaged by our present
undertaking. Holding this faith and this larger hope, but
not waiting for its full realization, we are convinced that we
should now form ourselves into an organic union; and that
our union must be so truly ecumenical in spirit and structure
that it may be not only a church united in itself but so mani-
festly inspired with a fervent desire and intention to be used
of God that it will bring about a more comprehensive union.

cal faith to which such a united church should bear witness, and propose a plan of union.

II. *The Common Faith*

Whereas: we desire to share as a common heritage the faith of the Christian church which has in times past and in our own time found expression in many historic and treasured statements;

Whereas: we share a common belief in God our Father: in Jesus Christ, his only Son, our Savior; in the Holy Spirit, our Guide and Comforter; in the Holy Catholic Church, through which God's eternal purpose of salvation is proclaimed and his Kingdom is come on earth; in the Scriptures of the Old and New Testaments as disclosing the Word of God for men, from which new light is evermore breaking forth for us and for our world; and in the life everlasting;

Whereas: the church is of God, and hears with a deepened sense of obligation the prayer of our Lord "that they all may be one, that the world may believe"; and

Whereas: having the same spirit and owning the same Lord, we recognize diversity of gifts, concerns and ministrations for whose exercise the freedom of the Christian man must always be assured in forms of worship, modes of operation, and ways of life;

Therefore: we the churches hereto assenting, convinced that we are acting under the guidance of the Holy Spirit, seeking union in Christ with that Christian liberty of conscience and organization which we now enjoy, do hereby unite in a visible body to be known as the United Church of Christ for the furtherance of the redemptive work of Christ in the world. The churches hereto assenting and hereafter thus united in such visible body do mutually covenant and agree upon a plan of union:

There follows detailed information about the local church, the ministry, the Presbytery, the Conference, the General-Council, and the Promotion of Work. This report concludes with the following statement:

We, the Conference on Church Union, offer the foregoing plan of union in the belief that ultimately such an organic union rests upon faith in one another and in the continuing guidance of the Holy Spirit. The achievement of a united church is a spiritual development as well as an organizational event. We make no claim to finality or perfection in the concept of such a church as is here set forth. We submit it in all humility to the several churches for their prayerful consideration, criticism, revision and, we dare to hope, their favorable action in the adoption of its substantive structure.

In its widespread consideration, we prayerfully trust that the proposed union may be approached and its study controlled, not by a too meticulous concern for minor or technical details, but by confidence in the Christian character, disposition and spirit of the other churches as well as one's own. If our union can be consummated in such an atmosphere of faith, many lesser matters may wisely be left for adjustment in the joyous experience of living together in one fold under one Shepherd.

—The Conference on Church Union.

SIGNIFICANT MOVEMENTS OUTSIDE THE CHURCHES

Two movements deserve our consideration.

Protestants and Other Americans United for the Separation of Church and State

An organization which came into being in 1947, entitled "Protestants and Other Americans United for the Separation of Church and State," or POAU for short, deserves our consideration here. The manifesto of POAU is in part as follows:

The officers and the widely representative National Advisory Council of this organization desire to speak frankly and clearly to the American people concerning the purpose for which this undertaking has been launched. Its single and only purpose is to assure the maintenance of the American principle of separation of church and state upon which the Federal Constitution guarantees religious liberty to all the people and all churches of this Republic. PROTESTANTS AND OTHER AMERICANS UNITED has been called into existence because this principle has been and is being violated, and threatened with further violation, in certain areas and by certain acts of both government and church. The plain meaning of the First Amendment to the Constitution, which forbids Congress to make any law "respecting an establishment of religion" has been obscured by specious propaganda tending to confuse the public mind as to the clear-cut line of separation which this Amendment draws between church and state. We shall endeavor (1) to revive in the public mind a clear understanding of the constitutional basis upon which religious liberty has been guaranteed, (2) to redress the specific violations which have recently come into force, and (3) to resist further encroachments upon this constitutional principle.

PROTESTANTS AND OTHER AMERICANS UNITED does not concern itself with the religious teaching, the forms of worship, or the ecclesiastical organization of the many churches in our country. It is no part of our purpose to propagandize the Protestant faith or any other, nor to criticize or oppose the teaching or internal practices of the Roman Catholic Church or any other. It has no connection or sympathy with any movement that is tinged with religious fanaticism. Its motivation arises solely from patriotic and religious concern for the maintenance of the separation of church and state under the American form of government.

The immediate objectives of this organization are clearly stated:

1. To enlighten and mobilize public opinion in support of religious liberty as this monumental principle of democracy has been embodied and implemented in the Constitution by the separation of church and state.

2. To resist every attempt by law or the administration of

law further to widen the breach in the wall of separation of church and state.

3. To demand the immediate discontinuance of the ambassadorship to the papal head of the Roman Catholic Church.

4. To work for the repeal of any law now on the statute books of any state which sanctions the granting of aid to church schools from the public school treasury.

5. To invoke the aid of the courts in maintaining the integrity of the Constitution with respect to the separation of church and state, wherever and in whatever form the issue arises, and specifically, to strive by appropriate constitutional means to secure a reconsideration of the two decisions of the Supreme Court upholding the use of tax funds (a) for providing the pupils of parochial schools with free textbooks and (b) for the transportation of pupils to parochial schools.

6. To call out and unite all patriotic citizens in a concerted effort to prevent the passage of any law by Congress which allots to church schools any portion of a Federal appropriation for education or which explicitly or implicitly permits the State to make such allotment of Federal funds. This purpose in no wise prejudices pro or con the propriety of a Federal grant in aid of public education.

7. To give all possible aid to the citizens of any community or state who are seeking to protect their public schools from sectarian domination, or resisting any other assault upon the principle of separation of church and state.

8. In seeking these objectives we are determined to pursue a course that cannot be justly characterized as anti-Catholic, or as motivated by anti-Catholic animus. As Protestants, we can be called anti-Catholic only in the sense in which every Roman Catholic is anti-Protestant. Profound differences separate us in the area of religious faith, but these differences have no relevancy in the pursuit of our objectives as clearly defined in this manifesto. The issue of separation of church and state has arisen in the political area, and we propose to meet it there.

The separation of Church and State is basic in the American System. Neither must control the other; the Church should not control the State; neither should the State control the Church. Both the Church and the State have important stakes in maintaining the principle of separation, but that does not mean that governmental policy should not be tested by them in the light of their Christian convictions. The Church is the conscience of the State. The Church must be free from the State in order to be the conscience of the State. When the Church and the State fall out completely, it is ill with the State; when the Church and the State get along too well together, there is something wrong with the Church. One of the towering demands of the present crisis is that this should be done intelligently and effectively, without any side-stepping and with a clearness that will enable the individual and the group to wish to impose discipline upon themselves for their own good and for the well-being of all.

The National Conference of Christians and Jews

Another organization, the National Conference of Christians and Jews, has earnestly endeavored to bring Catholics, Protestants and Jews together into a co-operative interfaith movement. It was started in 1926 and, under the dynamic leadership of its national president, Dr. Everett R. Clinchy, it has had an astonishing growth. Approximately 300 people are employed in the 65 offices throughout the nation, and the budget raised in 1950 was approximately $1,600,000. The organization has had a tremendous appeal to many people, laymen, priests, rabbis and clergy, who have supported it with their money and time.

Some Protestants question the validity of its purpose, because of the lack of reciprocity on the part of the Roman Catholic Church, especially the hierarchy. They also claim that the Protestants who join must compromise their faith, whereas the other parties fail or refuse to make any concessions. Despite these objections, the National Conference has done splendid work in the field of interfaith relations, group relations and world brotherhood.

The other churches in the world stalwartly refuse to acknowledge that the Roman Church has a monopoly on God. Protestants have no intention of ever going back to unite with Rome. They repudiate absolutely the "authority" of the Roman Catholic Church, proclaiming that this church which claims the word "Catholic" as its exclusive right is the least qualified to use it, judged by its faith and practice. Tension between the Protestants and the Roman Catholics has been intensified of late, particularly on the part of laymen, because of the recent decision of the Vatican concerning membership by Roman Catholics in Rotary International.

COUNCILS OR FEDERATIONS OF CHURCHES

A movement of promise has taken form in Councils, or Federations, of Churches, which are now active in over 700 cities and counties in the United States. Most of these are unified councils or federations of churches, organized to replace councils of religious education or Sunday-school associations, and sometimes other interdenominational agencies as well. The term *council* is more commonly used than *federation*.

Generally speaking, these agencies for interdenominational co-operation have developed opportunistically and atomistically, and largely by accretion rather than according to a consciously formulated strategy of Protestant churchmanship. Interdenominational co-operation has grown up around specific functions and in terms of specific needs. Nondenominational co-operation in the area of Sunday-school work, the Christian associations (YMCA and YWCA) and Christian

Endeavor in the youth field paved the way for more formal ecclesiastical working together. Even official co-operation began with the functional boards—foreign and home missions, education—and not with the official denominational bodies themselves. In a few instances official co-operation on the local level began before the organization of the Federal Council of the Churches of Christ in America, but most federations started after 1907.

The commitments of the denominations to the principle of Christian unity are much deeper now than they were even a decade ago. But realistic facing of facts makes it clear that the denominations still have many reservations when it comes to specific expressions of this principle. They have not surrendered their sovereignty to interdenominational agencies. The denominations consider themselves to be the only competent ecclesiastical agencies in the matters of faith and order: i.e., in the administration of the sacraments, ordination, ordering the policy and life of local churches, the extension of the Church's life into home or foreign areas, carrying forward the vital functions of the Christian movement and formulating the faith of the Church.

Interdenominational agencies are given responsibilities in certain areas of life and work. Chiefly these areas are on the community level where co-ordination of denominational activities is required or where there are needs which require a corporate approach by the denominations or local churches; that is, where no single local church or denomination can meet the need alone.

These limitations must be kept in mind when a statement regarding the essential nature of a church federation is proposed. The range of possibilities for meeting real needs in the community is so great that interdenominational agencies have a large and significant place in the strategy of Protestantism even now. There is much to be gained in sharply limiting the functions of councils to fit the realities of denominational commitments.

The best way of recognizing these limitations and at the same time providing a positive interpretation is to think of a council or a church federation as a partnership of the denominations which have created it. It is analogous to a business partnership which is organized by two or more people for specific purposes agreed on by the partners. They retain independence in personal matters except those involved in the partnership itself. They are not required to marry the same woman, drive the same automobile, live in the same house, belong to the same political party or have the same religion. Partners may withdraw from one another by agreement, but as long as they are together they are responsible for one another and to one another within the limits of the partnership.

So it is with the denominations and the organizations created for interdenominational co-operation. Within this framework the denominations may expand their range of interest and common responsibilities without limit; and since such expansion must be by agreement, it will be normal and satisfactory to all concerned. Furthermore, the full power of Protestant Christianity will be generated because advance steps will have to be based on thorough education.

The concept of partnership does not limit councils in accomplishing their present tasks. Its greatest value is that it keeps the denominations and their interdenominational agencies in proper relationship to one another. At the same time it strengthens the relationships of denominations with their councils, which become the denominations' official societies for interdenominational action in community affairs. The councils become entitled to the same status and treatment in the denominations as are given their other official societies of home or foreign missions. Rather than "super" organizations or "superchurches" they become integrated into the official

life of the member denominations as a normal expression of
their lives.

The idea of partnership will limit those who advocate that
a church federation should be a full-fledged expression of
Christian unity, or that a federation's chief function should
be the prophetic one of crusading for complete unity. The
fact is that such people are very unrealistic about the extent
to which the denominations have actually committed themselves by entering into interdenominational relationships. But
councils do have a very great significance for Christian unity,
because a new formula is being developed from the fellowship
and experience of the councils and federations. This formula
is sure to have a profound effect on the nature of ultimate
Christian unity. It is the idea of unity *with freedom*. Whatever may be said about the limitations of denominationalism,
it must be admitted that the denominational pattern of Protestantism is an expression of the principle of religious freedom. Through interdenominational co-operation Protestants
are realizing that it is possible to have functional unity without sacrificing freedom. The authoritarian dogmatism, which
is implicit in the traditional behavior of most Protestant denominations and which was carried over from Roman Catholicism, is being dissolved slowly by the actual experience of
fellowship. This experience, and the idea of unity *with freedom* which it is generating, are sure to be written large into
the final plan for organic Christian unity.

My thanks are due to Dr. John W. Harms, the Executive
Vice-President of the Church Federation of Greater Chicago,
for furnishing me with factual material and interpretations
concerning a church federation.

A church federation conceived as a partnership of denominations and limited as has been noted has the following
objectives:

  1. To give expression to the inherent unity which the

communions and their local churches have in a common loyalty to Jesus Christ;

2. To develop a real sense of fellowship which is both spiritual and temporal through the promotion of Christian activity which will take the Christian message to the individual and corporate life of the people and promote its application in all their relationships;

3. To provide such co-operative and co-ordinated leadership as the member bodies agree is needed, that there may be the maximum use of all denominational resources without wasteful competition;

4. To assume such corporate spiritual ministries as are declared by the member bodies to be their common responsibilities; and

5. To interpret the moral and social problems of the community to the member bodies and to mobilize their resources for solving such problems.

The first objective recognizes the obligation of a church federation to express the greatest reality in Christianity, its inherent unity. The preamble of the revised constitution of the Church Federation of Greater Chicago, for example, expresses it thus:

Recognizing that in God's universe variety and unity are in harmonious relation we, the member bodies of this Federation, declare that likewise among us there is inherent in our variety and freedom of faith and order an unbreakable unity which has its basis in a common loyalty to Jesus Christ and which we must express in cooperative activity in matters of life and work.

The second objective emphasizes the place of fellowship in the Christian Church and among the denominations, a fellowship which grows out of a common Christian faith and common causes.

The third and fourth objectives state specifically the two types of Christian activity which are proper for federations to undertake, and they provide a standard by which to determine the kind of leadership required in meeting any specific need.

The fifth objective states the church federation's basic responsibility for the two-way process of education and action in community leadership. Out of this process will come the specific proposals to be measured against the objectives three and four.

When these five objectives are made the form of adequacy for councils there will be less trouble with the problem of duplication between councils and denominations. Some councils will drop certain functions and take on others. In many instances problems will disappear regarding functions about which there is now difficulty because they are set in a new framework of understanding and agreement brought about by rethinking the situation.

The strategy of the Christian Church in its total expression of life may be said to have the following five basic elements: Fellowship, Education, Worship, Evangelism and Social Action. In a real sense these are the basic elements in the functioning of a church federation if it expresses the total strategy of the Christian Church in the corporate life of the community. They will be valuable, however, only as they are used as a frame of reference in which to set a much more specific analysis of what is required if Protestantism is to be an effective corporate Christian movement. The following interdenominational functions are certainly among those required if this need is to be met. They should be carried on through the church federation.

There must be statesmanlike planning for the establishment of new churches, and for the relocation of churches as needed to meet shifting population trends. This course of procedure commonly called *comity* should be refined greatly as the churches face the ever-shifting conditions of the future. The aim should be to make available to all with a Protestant heritage or who are a Protestant responsibility, the opportunity to have the fellowship of a local church and its ministry of worship, education and pastoral service.

There should be such co-ordination of the denominational evangelistic efforts in the community as will make sure that every person for whom Protestant churches are responsible has brought to him systematically and consistently the claims of religion upon him and his family.

There should be an interdenominational plan for providing universally the basic religious teaching required for the preservation of the religious foundations of our democratic civilization. Likewise, there should be a common plan whereby liaison relationships of co-operation and mutual interpretation are established between the churches and the institutions of public education. Protestant churches should provide an adequate agency of investigation which will furnish them with the facts about the social and religious conditions of the community's life, and their responsibility for meeting these human needs.

The range of specific activities within these functions of a church federation show two variations:

Co-ordination functions: where the council is responsible for co-ordinating the activities of the denominations for greater total effectiveness. In such instances the denominations plan jointly but assume primary administrative responsibility for carrying out the project.

Corporate ministries: where responsibility for both planning and actual administration is vested in the council because no one local church or denomination can effectively administer the program.

THE FEDERAL COUNCIL OF CHURCHES

Co-operation on a federal basis has been carried on for over forty years, "long enough to have developed a spirit of mutual trust, a sense of the inner unity of Protestantism, and a strong purpose." In the Federal Council of Churches of Christ in America constituent denominations were banded together "for the prosecution of work that can be done better in union than in separation."

Until November 1950 the Federal Council of the Churches of Christ in America was the accredited agency through which 27 national denominations, comprising nearly 150,000 local congregations with a total communicant membership of over 28,000,000, joined together in common tasks. It was the central instrument through which these otherwise separated bodies came into a united witness to their central Christian convictions and united service in undertakings that could be carried out together better than separately.

The Council was strengthened by four decades of testing after its creation in 1908. It grew steadily in influence and effectiveness. It held a unique place as the greatest movement of Christian unity in our national life, until the newly formed National Council replaced it.

The Federal Council was the direct creation of the churches themselves. It had a carefully drawn constitution, officially ratified by the highest authority of the churches that comprised its membership.

The objectives of the Federal Council, as defined in its constitution were:

1. To express the fellowship and catholic unity of the Christian Church.

2. To bring the Christian bodies of America into united service for Christ and the world.

3. To encourage devotional fellowship and mutual counsel concerning the spiritual life and religious activities of the Churches.

4. To secure a larger combined influence for the Churches in all matters affecting the moral and social condition of the people, so as to promote the application of the law of Christ in every relation of human life.

All churches which share the basic faith in Jesus Christ as "Divine Lord and Saviour" were eligible to membership. Into the details of doctrine the Council did not enter, its function being practical rather than theoretical. It had no separate creed of its own but stood firmly on the great historic confessions of faith of the groups which comprised it.

Although made up primarily of Protestant constituents the Federal Council was organized on a basis broad enough to welcome all branches of historical Christianity which are committed to the ideal of fellowship and the practice of co-operation with other churches. Beginning in 1938 four Eastern Orthodox groups were received into membership.

The following churches were related to the Federal Council when it merged into the National Council of Churches:

Northern Baptist Convention
National Baptist Convention
Church of the Brethren
Congregational Christian Churches
Czech-Moravian Brethren
Disciples of Christ
Evangelical United Brethren Church
Evangelical and Reformed Church
Methodist Church
African Methodist Episcopal Church
African Methodist Episcopal Zion Church
Colored Methodist Episcopal Church in America

Moravian Church
Presbyterian Church in U.S.
Presbyterian Church in U.S.A.
Protestant Episcopal Church
Reformed Church in America
Religious Society of Friends Five Years Meeting
Religious Society of Friends of Philadelphia and Vicinity
Roumanian Orthodox Church of America
Russian Orthodox Church in North America
Seventh Day Baptist General Conference
Syrian Antiochian Orthodox Church of North America
Ukrainian Orthodox Church of America
United Church of Canada
United Lutheran Church
United Lutheran Church (Consultative)
United Presbyterian Church

So we, being many, are one body in Christ, and every one members one of another (Romans 12:5).

As the Federal Council was officially created by the churches, so also was it wholly responsible to them. Organized on a strictly representative principle, it was governed by approximately 400 delegated representatives, all named directly by the constituent denominations. These representatives in their annual meetings constituted a central board of interdenominational strategy, developing a common mind, planning united policies and providing for concerted action. In the interim, an executive committee, made up of 85 members, all of whom also directly represented the co-operating churches and were selected by those churches, met bimonthly for the supervision of the Council's work.

The genius of the Council was to foster a united spiritual fellowship which expressed itself in many lines of united action. It had no legislative authority over the denominations and was in no sense a super organization, but through its representative character and its democratic processes it federated the churches themselves and co-ordinated their programs. It conserved freedom and diversity, with no thought of dictation or enforced uniformity, at the same time that it secured a needed unity in action.

During the years in which the national denominations were drawing together in this way, furthering the development of state and community councils was one of the most important responsibilities of the Federal Council. There were over 875 county and state Councils of Churches and of Religious Education, created by the Christian groups of their own communities, responsible for co-operative work there. In 40 states of the Union there were state-wide Councils of Churches providing leadership for a united Christian program.

No action could testify more eloquently to the increasing effectiveness of the Federal Council than did the attack upon it by John T. Flynn in Chapter X of *The Road Ahead*. This book has been widely circulated by an organization called the Committee for Constitutional Government.

A most able detailed factual analysis was prepared by the General Secretary of the Council, Dr. Samuel McCrea Cavert, and was part of a pamphlet called, *The Truth about the Federal Council of Churches*. The analysis is so pertinent that most of it is quoted here:

Whatever one may think of other parts of John T. Flynn's *The Road Ahead,* Chapter X, entitled "The Kingdom of God" is so replete with misunderstandings, misrepresentations and falsities that it is immediately apparent that the author is writing about a field with which he is wholly unfamiliar. It is not surprising that the *Reader's Digest,* in summarizing the book, did not include a single sentence from this chapter. The chapter is really a caricature of the Federal Council of the Churches of Christ in America.

To take an egregrious illustration, Mr. Flynn cites (Page

114) what is alleged to be a quotation from the "Social Creed of the Churches" about competition as "nothing more than a partially conventionalized embodiment of primeval selfishness." But the statement is not in the "Social Creed" at all! It is obvious that he has never even read the document which he is presuming to discuss. A footnote, in small type, at the bottom of the page indicates how he fell into such a blunder. He has accepted at its face value an intemperate and unreliable book by a man who was deposed from the ministry of the Presbyterian Church in the U.S.A., after full trial, on June 30, 1936, and who has since been engaged in a campaign of bitter attack upon that Church, upon other historic denominations, and upon the Federal Council of Churches, in which the denominations co-operate with one another.

This is the authority to whom Mr. Flynn's book refers again and again. Indeed, there is virtually nothing in Mr. Flynn's discussion of the Federal Council which is not found in the publications of the deposed Presbyterian minister, whose animus against the established churches and their agencies is easy to understand.

Since Mr. Flynn does not himself come from a Protestant background he must, of course, depend on some source other than his own knowledge. There would be no objection to his getting information anywhere if only it were not misinformation. But his chapter on the Churches is full of errors in even the most elemental matters. He talks, for example, about some powerful "policy committee," but there is no committee with such a name and only the Executive Committee, made up exclusively of the appointees of the denominations, determines policies. He says that an "American Council of Churches" was formed when a "small group of clergymen broke away from the Federal Council," although the fact is that not a single one of the little denominations comprising the American Council ever belonged to the Federal Council.

Far more serious is Mr. Flynn's failure to understand what the Federal Council is or to indicate its true nature. He is so confused that he contradicts himself. He refers on page 107 to "the organization of a clique of Christian ministers and laymen," and on page 112 describes the Council as "the greatest religious lay body in America." Obviously it cannot be both. The fact is that it is neither. It is an official federation of national denominations, whose members are named entirely by the highest authority of those denominations. Its programs and policies are regularly reported to all the national assemblies and conferences of the member denominations, are subject to review and are often the subject of extensive discussion.

Mr. Flynn finally reaches the stage of the ridiculous as well as of the confused when on page 118 he describes the Methodist Church as "controlled by the men who are foremost in control of the Federal Council." The nine million people of the Methodist Church will be amused to learn who "controls" them!

In his treatment of certain individuals Mr. Flynn parrots the loose charges which the deposed Presbyterian minister on whom he relies has long been making and with the same kind of distortions. He blames Bishop Oxnam, for example, for having sponsored Soviet-American friendship rallies but fails to point out that this was during World War II, when Russia was officially the ally of America and it was a matter of patriotism to co-operate with our allies, and that he discontinued his relation to the Soviet-American program when conditions changed after the war. Mr. Flynn alleges that Bishop Oxnam "is a Socialist" but the Bishop declares, "I am not now and never have been a Socialist." . . .

Not only the nature of the Federal Council, but its program is grossly misrepresented. No one could guess from reading Mr. Flynn's book that the Council was formed more than forty years ago as the result of efforts to secure an effective co-operation among otherwise separated denominations. No one could guess that it is today the chief influence for a greater unity in Protestantism. No one could guess from Mr. Flynn's account that the Council is the instrument of the co-operating Churches for co-ordinating their evangelistic work, and that the budget of its Department of Evangelism is larger than any other. No one could guess that it has for decades functioned in such basic fields as the devotional life and worship, pastoral counseling, religion and health, Christian family life and religious broadcasting as well as in relation to social and international responsibilities. Mr. Flynn gives a grossly false perspective on the Council.

In policy, as well as in program, he misrepresents the Council. He declares, for example, that "Article Five of the Social Creed . . . demands socialized medicine." But he is careful never to cite the article, for to do so would show how erroneous his statement is. What Article Five really advocates, as a means of protection against the unexpected hazards of life, is "social insurance against sickness or accident, want in old age, and unemployment." This was written in 1932, after our country had gone through the terrible years of unemployment and suffering. Today some form of social insurance against accident, against want in old age and against unemployment is taken for granted. . . .

It will be noted that most of Mr. Flynn's quotations from Federal Council statements go back to 1932. Why does he not quote from documents of today? Surely statements made in 1932 are to be understood in the light of the conditions of that time. It was a time when the most conservative men were urging our government to take a more active part in bringing about industrial recovery—a time very different from that of 1949-50. The Federal Council's position today is officially and fully set forth in a statement of 1948 entitled "Basic Christian Principles and Assumptions in Relation to the Church and Economic Life." Yet Mr. Flynn never even so much as mentions it.

Nor does he take any cognizance whatever of the Department of the Church and Economic Life, headed by President Arthur S. Flemming of Ohio Wesleyan University, former Chairman of the U. S. Civil Service Commission. It is this group, including Christian leaders in business, management, labor and agriculture, which is responsible for developing the Federal Council's policies in the economic field. Why does Mr. Flynn ignore it? Obviously because a description of its work and statements would show the hollowness of his charges.

At the beginning of the chapter he says he will discuss conditions in "the Churches" but he limits his discussion to Protestantism. He speaks only of the branch of Christianity which is not his own. Yet all thoughtful students of the relation of the American Churches to social and industrial affairs know that the policies of the National Catholic Welfare Conference in this field show a striking parallelism with those of the Federal Council. The bulletin entitled "The Yardstick," published by the National Catholic Welfare Conference, in its issue of November 14, 1949, vigorously defends the Federal Council against Mr. Flynn and identifies itself with the Federal Council's position. It says in part:

> This is the most emotional, illogical, inaccurate and probably even libelous book which we have ever been foolish enough to purchase. . . . Mr. Flynn does well to warn the American public about the dangers of Socialism and about the possibility of our drifting into Socialism unconsciously, as it were, and in spite of our good intentions. By the same token, however, he does a great disservice to the American reading public by indiscriminately fastening the label "socialistic" on a lot of organizations and programs which have yet to become as "radical" (his word) as—well, as the social encyclicals, for example . . . Mr. Flynn, in his chapter on the Churches and Socialism, concentrates his fire on the Federal Council of Churches of Christ in America and never so much as mentions the word Catholic. Perhaps he realized that it would be difficult, if not impossible, to persuade his readers that Pope Pius XI was a Socialist.

> The most serious aspect of the chapter is the implication that if the Churches, prompted by the Christian conscience, actively support any measures of social justice and human welfare they are thereby helping to undermine the American way of life and to deliver our country to ultimate domination by the Communists. Mr. Flynn apparently cannot see that to bring about constructive measures of social advance is the way to prevent Communism, not to further it. He often creates the impression that to correct injustices, to defend the rights of minority groups, to be concerned with poverty and unemployment, to seek greater co-operation in our economic and industrial life, to try sincerely to hold up all our

social practices to the light of the Christian Gospel, these things are synonymous with Socialism and lead to Communism. If Christian people should come to believe this, it would be a disaster to our nation.

So unfair an attack did not affect to any real extent the work and support of the Federal Council. Naturally some contributions from businessmen were curtailed, but the work of the extended organization was too well established to be affected. Thank God, "no lie can live forever!" Even a few short weeks were sufficient to correct statements of an author whose chief aim seems to have been to write a "best seller."

We are living in demanding days which are testing the belief and hope of every concerned person capable of thinking for himself. We live in a world where "the pillars of civilization are creaking and tilting," as John Buchan vividly states in his book *Memory Hold the Door,* an observation that is persistently haunting the minds of thoughtful people. It is an accepted truth that these are the days that are measuring to the last limits the Christian optimism of every intelligent person.

To be told in pulpit and in books "How to Adjust," "How to Relax," "How to Stop Worrying and Start Living," "How to Have Peace of Mind," is definitely not enough. Moreover, it is positively dangerous as it tends to make us indifferent to our own basic weaknesses and sins. Our great need is to have an awakened conscience through the revival of a well-developed moral sense based on a theology which is historically true, a theology that has borne the test and resistance of individual and social experience. The demand is for a theology to live by, a theology that will not lead us in the wrong direction, but in the right direction. We cannot have a new moral sense without a vital religion—a religion that guides, disciplines, dominates, elevates and redeems our lives individually and collectively. This, the Protestant Church, at its best, offers to man.

Nothing else can suffice for the future world which stands teetering on the brink of disintegration and destruction. There is dire need for a continuing reformation—no doubt along new lines. The reason is obvious—the world is too strong for a divided Church. Therefore this new reformation will assist in the unity of the churches into an ecumenical Church, and make fresh the sense of the truth that "our field is the world."

It is significant that Protestant Christianity has become in recent years and for the first time, in any realistic sense, a world religion. Only Christian unity in things of the spirit can help us to fulfill the role which destiny has placed in our hands. It is an established truth that "united we stand, divided we fall." The past fifty years have witnessed a real advance in the area of Protestant Church co-operation. It is greater than the sum total of the previous eighteen centuries. It has been effected largely through the efforts of great souls, both of the clergy and laity, who have come together for consultation and mutual aid.

THE NATIONAL COUNCIL OF THE CHURCHES OF CHRIST IN THE UNITED STATES OF AMERICA

An experiment of great significance has recently been launched. After years of study, twelve interdenominational bodies merged into the National Council of the Churches of Christ in the United States of America at a constitutional convention held at Cleveland, Ohio, in November 1950. This Council developed from the uniting of the following twelve agencies:

The Federal Council of the Churches of Christ in America
The Foreign Missions Conference of North America
The Home Missions Council of North America
The International Council of Religious Education
The Missionary Education Movement of the United States
   and Canada
The National Protestant Council of Higher Education
The United Council of Church Women
The United Stewardship Council
The Protestant Radio Commission
The Protestant Film Commission
The Church World Service
The Inter-Seminary Movement

The preamble of the constitution presented at the convention reads as follows:

In the Providence of God, the time has come when it seems fitting more fully to manifest oneness in Jesus Christ as Divine Lord and Savior, by the creation of an inclusive co-operative agency of the Christian churches of the United States of America to continue and extend the preceding general agencies of the churches and to combine all their interests and functions. . . .

Each denomination retains full freedom whether or not it will support the National Council of Churches. Every delegate to a convention must be a member of a denomination which supports it and must be so certified by denominational authorities.

The creation of this new national co-operative agency was voted officially in June 1950 by 25 of the great religious denominations of the United States, including most of the leading Protestant and the Eastern Orthodox communions. It is designed to give added power and effectiveness to the Christian forces in our American life.

The National Council is one great Protestant and Orthodox agency and it will deal with the Christian tasks and
problems which concern the nation as a whole. Ten reasons
for the Council are as follows:

1. This generation faces overwhelming problems and dis-
ruptive forces that challenge the total efforts of the Christian
Church.

2. The Council gives a channel for more than 27,000,000
church members to work together to meet that challenge.

3. Twenty-five denominations are already dedicated to one
essential purpose—to make Christ known, loved and served
throughout the world.

4. Co-operation provides maximum mutual encouragement
and support in the pursuit of common objectives.

5. A central co-operative agency facilitates the best use
of personnel, time and energy for strategic consultations.

6. It focuses the best insights of Christian men and women
on critical areas of moral and spiritual concern.

7. Effective integration accomplishes far more than unco-
ordinated actions.

8. Protestant Christians can speak more effectively with a
common voice through the press, radio and other mass media.

9. It will encourage more effective co-operation of Christian forces in local community life.

10. It is a significant step toward the fulfillment of Christ's
prayer for his followers: "That they all may be one."

Until the nineteenth century, Protestantism was concerned
mainly with carrying out the Reformation principle of freedom for the individual and the group. Then the resultant
separate churches began to feel their common responsibility
for missionary enterprise and an ethical impact upon the total
community. The immensity of the task and the weakness of
unrelated attempts to master it have led to steadily increasing
efforts to provide maximum mutual encouragement and sup-

port through co-operation without surrendering the right to differ among themselves in minor matters of creed and polity.

Significantly, the first known instance of such activity in America was when a group of laymen in 1832 held a National Sunday School Convention on an interdenominational basis for mutual helpfulness and inspiration. This was the forerunner of the International Council of Religious Education (1872) which today maintains a vast and many-sided program aimed to bring children, youth and adults into Christian discipleship. A pattern of consultation already set on many foreign mission fields led to the establishment of the Foreign Missions Conference of North America in 1893 and a series of ecumenical missionary conferences beginning in 1900.

The Missionary Education Movement of the United States and Canada was organized by home and foreign mission boards in 1902. In 1908 the Federal Council of the Churches of Christ in America was organized by the denominations themselves, and related to it there have since developed nearly 900 city, county and state councils of churches. Functional co-operation has been advanced by the formation of the Home Missions Council of North America in 1908, the National Protestant Council of Higher Education in 1911 and the United Stewardship Council in 1920, all founded by denominational boards to make their work more effective. Finally there came into being the United Council of Church Women in 1941, joining the specialized women's activities of the national bodies with the development of activity among women in their home localities.

This is not enough. As these co-operative agencies evolved their programs from the point of view of their own special fields, they found overlappings and uncertain divisions of responsibility, particularly among these serving in the United States. Co-operative action has been found to be effective, and also to be rich in reflected benefits to local churches and communities in support of their own aims and undertakings. Out of the total experience has come the conviction that still more can be gained by uniting all these agencies of the denominations into one council, with the same functions provided for and clearly assigned to different units within the whole.

Great unfinished tasks await us as we enter the second half of the "fabulous twentieth century," calling for the mobilization of all our spiritual insights and energies. For example, there are 15,000,000 boys and girls between the ages of five and seven not reached by religious education, which has been declared the most effective means for fighting juvenile delinquency. At least 5,000 new Protestant church buildings and 10,000 new church-school buildings are required if we are to have even minimum standards of space and equipment for our Christian worship, education and service. Many of these must be in new population centers. There are 700 community or residential developments, each containing at least 2,500 persons, which have not as yet a single church. In more general terms, such areas of life as the home and family, labor relationships, economic issues, inter-racial fellowship, missionary responsibility, a deeper sense of stewardship, international justice and good will, and a true and lasting world peace all demand the co-ordination of our best efforts.

Feeling the urgency of our Christian calling, leaders of our co-operative agencies for the past nine years explored the possibilities of still closer unity of administration and action for greater effectiveness in the task of enriching the spiritual meaning and contents of modern life. This called for vision and skill of a high order, as well as devotion to the ideal. Each agency, each denomination studied the proposals and gave its approval.

It was a great moment in religious history as a representative of each of 25 major Protestant and four Eastern Orthodox churches signed constituting documents, and then heard the presiding officer, Dr. Franklin Clark Fry of New York, formally declare the National Council "officially constituted."

The capstone in the arch of co-operative Christianity in America was erected in a memorable ceremony in snowbound Cleveland's public auditorium Wednesday morning, November 29. Against the backdrop of the banners of the 29 constituent denominations the eight merging agencies signified that they now were united in an interchurch enterprise linking 3,000,000 Christians in 150,000 churches across the land.

There were 4,000 delegates present as the plan for one great interdenominational agency became a reality. At one table near the front sat a group with a special interest in the moment. It was the planning committee of 48 men and women—six from each of the merging agencies—who in large measure were the architects of the National Council. Most of them had been at Atlantic City in 1941 when the blueprint for such an organization was first conceived. Now they were witnessing the harvest of their years of arduous and intensive efforts.

Every step necessary to enable the National Council to start operations was taken during the historic four-day meeting—the first general assembly, as well as the constituting convention, of the new council of churches. The delegates chose as the first president a distinguished clergyman—the Right Reverend Henry Knox Sherrill of Greenwich, Connecticut, the presiding bishop of the Protestant Episcopal Church. In his presidential address, Bishop Sherrill characterized the formation of the National Council as a "promise of high hope for the future."

Then he added: "The churches here represented are de-

termined without compromise to co-operate wholeheartedly
in those great fields of endeavor in which we are essentially
one."

Calling the times "stern," and labeling the forces of evil
"powerful and relentless," the newly elected president condemned "laissez faire" Christianity without dynamic force as
inadequate. "Only a Church of deep conviction and spiritual
experience," he emphasized, "can meet the necessities of our
times. . . .

"The real Problem which confronts our churches is not
the strength of the enemy without, but the quality of the
spiritual life within. The council can only be strong as the
churches are strong."

These delegates named as the chief administrative officer,
of a staff of more than 400, Dr. Samuel McCrea Cavert,
general secretary of the Federal Council of Churches. Dr.
Cavert was elected general secretary; and Dr. Roy G. Ross,
general secretary of the International Council of Religious
Education, was elected associate general secretary. A budget
that will exceed $4,435,000 was presented and the interim
policy-making body—a 100-member General Board—was
formally constituted and held two sessions. Temporarily the
National Council's offices are decentralized in several buildings in New York, and the ICRE building in Chicago. The
administrative offices are at 297 Fourth Avenue, New York.

The creation of the National Council of Churches is a significant step toward greater co-operative unity. A co-operative movement that includes some 25,000,000 people representing 29 different denominations cannot be said to be hopelessly divided. Can we demonstrate to the world that we may
get all the values of unity by voluntarily working together?
Can we demonstrate that while gaining our freedom, we can
also win the spirit of unity? It may well be that the successful
conducting of this experiment will decide the destiny of

America and of democratic institutions throughout the world. Can unity be the will of free people under God, or must it be based on regimented human authority? This is the question that a Protestant must face and answer honestly and convincingly if one is to bear fruitful witness to the claim: "I am a Protestant."

8

THE WORLD IS OUR FIELD

OUR world is split up into fragmentary and conflicting individuals and groups, but Protestant Christians in nearly every service of worship pray the Lord's Prayer, which emphasizes "Our Father . . . our daily bread . . . our debts . . . our debtors." The word is "our." We have a divine mandate: "Go ye therefore, and teach all nations, baptizing them in the name of the Father, and of the Son, and of the Holy Ghost . . ." (Matthew 28:19). The world is our field. Only Christian unity can help us obey this command and fulfill the role which destiny has placed in our hands. Granted that "the world is our field," the question is: How can we become a co-operative community rather than a warring world? That is the question of questions.

THE WORLD COUNCIL OF CHURCHES

One of the most significant events in the first half of the present century was the meeting of the World Council of Churches. In August 1948 the first official meeting of this body was held in Amsterdam with representatives from 147 denominations, Protestant, Orthodox and Old Catholics, from 44 nations. The theme of the gathering was a most wisely selected one—namely, "Man's Disorder and God's Design." It sought to establish an Ecumenical Church.

Ecumenical, ecumenicity, ecumenics—what mouth-filling words! Enthusiasts in the movement which the words describe have even been dubbed *ecumaniacs!* One wit—his identity is disputed—has said that "the word ecumenical is phonetically execrable and psychologically questionable, but etymologically incontestable, theologically respectable and logically inevitable!"

Is it "logically inevitable"? *Yes!* It has its roots in Christian history, for *ecumenical* stems directly from the Greek word by which the earliest councils of the Christian Church were named. It describes the present movement toward Christian unity accurately, because it long ago came to mean the "whole household of God," all nations, all branches of the Church throughout all the world or, as the familiar hymn puts it, "all people that on earth do dwell." On the other hand, it has never been used, like the word *catholic,* to refer to any particular branch of the Church. Finally, the best minds in Christendom have sought for another word as fitting and can find no other as adequate or meaningful.

. . . What is the Church? Where is the Church? And what and where is *ecumenical?* Let us see.

In the first place, *ecumenical* is one of the most intriguing and poignant of words. It is, of course, much more than a word. Weighted with history, it is discovery, achievement and adventure. Many people don't know the word. And if they do, the majority are unaware of its range, power and possibilities. To those who do know, however, the ecumenical not only means "the great new fact of our time," it is hope in the face of despair, it is world-wide unity in the midst of division, it is purpose and order where chaos confuses, it is fundamental to peace.

The word *ecumenical* means, literally, "pertaining to the inhabited world," from the Greek *oikoumenikos* . . . denoting, according to *Webster's New International Dictionary,* "general; world-wide . . . Eccl.,* pertaining to, representing . . . the whole church; as, an ecumenical council."[1]

---

[1] Charles T. Leber (ed.), *World Faith in Action*, p. 18. Copyright 1951, used by special permission of the publishers, The Bobbs-Merrill Company, Inc.

The aim broadly speaking is, of course, Christian unity. But those two words can stand for much or almost nothing! At one extreme, unity is conceived of in terms of *uniformity*—identity of creed, of forms of worships, of polity. That is the unity which marks the Roman Catholic Church and against which the Reformers rebelled. That decidedly is not the aim of the ecumenical movement. At the other extreme is a vague, shadowy ideal which has no living reality. We can sing lustily that "we are not divided, all one body we," but the world sees little evidence of it! A body without a spirit is a corpse, but "spirit without a body is a ghost."

In ecumenicity we are seeking for a unity without uniformity, marked by a diversity that is not divisiveness. The Church in New Testament times did not have uniformity. St. Paul gloried in the fact that there were differences of gifts, of operations, of ministrations. There were various forms of church government—or lack of it—in his day. But there was a unity of spirit and of action, too, which made the churches one as over against the secular world outside. It was said of them that "what the soul is to the body, Christians are in the world . . . it is they who hold the world together." Thus greatly did their unity impress an observer in the second century. It cannot yet be said of the twentieth.

The foundation or basis on which ecumenicity is built is the conviction that God wills unity in Christ. That conviction, in turn, is derived from the Bible and from Christian history and experience. The Bible is the book of the Church. We find the "charter of the ecumenical Church" in St. Paul's letter to the Ephesians. The first chapter states that God "has made known to us in all wisdom and insight the mystery of His will, according to His purpose which he set forth in Christ as a plan for the fullness of time, to unite all things in Him, things in heaven and things on earth." And toward the end of the chapter he describes God's placing of Christ far above all rule and authority, and making him the head over all things for the Church which is his body!

If the Church is the body of Christ, that corporate body which is to do in the world what the living body of Christ did when in the flesh, then it is obvious that it is one body even though it has many members. "If we are walking with Christ then we must be walking with each other." So wrote Bishop Brent, one of the pioneers of the ecumenical movement. And it is a perilous thing for one to judge that he is walking with Christ while his Christian brother of another branch of the Church is not. If we all had perfect vision there would be no division. The trouble comes when men mistake their small segment of the truth for the whole truth.

So much for the basis in terms of underlying principles. The basis which is set forth in the constitution of the World Council of Churches, and to which the constituent churches have assented, is thus expressed: "a fellowship of Churches which accept our Lord Jesus Christ as God and Saviour." The doctrinal phrase is a historic one and emphasizes the fact that unity is to be found in Christ as men have a common relatedness to him. Then note the word *fellowship*. The statement is often made that the World Council of Churches is based on the "federal" system of unity. That is not so, for in the federal system a very large measure of autonomy is surrendered by the parts to the whole. The World Council is simply an organized fellowship. The complete autonomy of its members is preserved. The charge that it is intended to be a "superchurch" has no ground either in its founding or in its nearly ten years of "formative" experience.

The World Council starts with all the richness of content possessed by the two world movements which have merged to form the Council—"The Universal Christian Council for Life and Work" and the "World Conference on Faith and Order." The constitution itself provides that its functions shall be, first of all, to carry on the work of those movements. During the years of formation it has discharged, in an ever-expanding program, the "Life and Work" task of a ministry to the victims of war, in maintaining orphaned missions and in keeping open Christian communications on both sides of the battle lines. In wide areas of agreement it has acted for the churches, accomplishing things in unity which could not have been done in separation. The field is almost limitless, for it becomes clearer every day that the "world is too strong for a divided Church." The relationship of the Christian to secular society, his responsibility as a citizen, his involvement in international affairs—all these are great and pressing problems which demand the pooling of abilities for study and, in the areas of agreement, common action.

More Christians are familiar with the "Life and Work" side of ecumenicity because they have experienced it in local, state and national councils of churches. They need to become acquainted with "Faith and Order" and its efforts to get Christians frankly to face their differences in an atmosphere of Christian fellowship, to probe the depths of problems of the nature of the Church and its mission in the world, to magnify the great common heritage which we all possess, to discover the "Church amid the churches."

"To promote the growth of ecumenical consciousness in the members of all Churches"—there is the meat of the matter. What a stupendous task—to develop within the churches Christians who are consciously members of a world-wide fellowship that knows no boundaries of geography, race, color or creed; membership in which is the most important relationship of life; a fellowship that cannot be disrupted by any earthly power and which is so much a "togetherness" that it can be the vital core which holds the world together!

After a provisional period of ten years, the World Council of Churches was organized at the Assembly in Amsterdam.

Its constitution provides for a permanent organization in which the constituent churches are officially represented, the administrative responsibility being lodged in a Central Committee of ninety, elected by the Assembly.

The sense of need for a working unity grew out of the missionary movement which, under God, has planted the Church in every nation. The idea of a world fellowship of churches took concrete form at two great ecumenical conferences: "Life and Work" (Stockholm, 1925) and "Faith and Order" (Lausanne, 1927). At Utrecht, in 1938, representatives elected at the world conferences of Oxford and Edinburgh (1937) elaborated plans for the World Council which were formally ratified at the Amsterdam World Assembly. The Council is not a "superchurch" and will have no jurisdiction over the church bodies associated with it.

Christ prayed four times for one thing: "That they all may be one."

Here is a clear mandate for Christian unity. During the past twenty-five years there has developed a marked trend toward the union (or reunion) of churches whose basic doctrines are not very different and whose divergences were accidental or even geographical rather than fundamental. On the other hand the historic ecclesiastical groupings into which Christianity has fallen have shown great tenacity in loyalty toward beliefs and tenets held to be vital. Yet most of the non-Roman churches now believe that "to take counsel together," to take a common stand on questions to which every Christian has substantially the same answer and to seek unified action in combatting evils and dangers which confront them all alike, is by no means incompatible with denominational independence and with the safeguarding of a sacred doctrinal trust. Unity is not uniformity.

The solid achievements of earlier co-operating Christian organizations, such as the International Missionary Council, the Christian Student Movement and the Federal Council of Churches, are a demonstration of the validity of this opinion. The idea of a World Council of Churches, however, goes beyond the earlier efforts to co-ordinate church life and work in various fields in that it is ecumenical—embracing "the whole household of the Christian faith . . . all races, all nations, all branches of the Church itself throughout the world." The organization of the World Council is an ecumenical step toward Christian unity, the crystallization of what has come to be generally known as the Ecumenical Movement.

If the world of nations is ever to achieve unity, Christianity must lead the way. If the Christian Church does not make itself heard in the present clamor of conflicting aims, the outlook for humanity is dark indeed. But to be heard and regarded, churches must speak together! All their strength of numbers and spiritual resources must be pooled in the effort to save mankind from disintegration and chaos, through achievement of spiritual world community. Every step toward union through fellowship or service with Christian groups constitutes a move in the right direction. Ecumenicity begins with a sense of identity and oneness among all Christians, and it can best begin in our local communities where churches and councils function. Christian unity at the top is not enough; it needs support by Christian co-operation and unity at the bottom.

What does the World Council—and the Ecumenical Movement generally speaking—mean to the individual church member? It means an extended horizon, an enlarged vision of a wide landscape, at once diversified and harmonious. A wall has crumbled away and a new land is spread out before our eyes. The degree to which the Christian churches will really win that new territory will depend on the wholehearted interest and vigorous participation of the congregation, or rather, of the people who make up the congregation. A few pioneers have gone forth to explore and have come back with a good report after long and careful reconnaissance. The follow-up must come from an enthusiastic Christian public: enthusiastic, because convinced that the unity of all the Christian forces of the world is a goal worth striving for; convinced, because it has taken the trouble to be thoroughly informed about the nature, history and aims of the effort to achieve Christian unity, which is acquiring concrete form in the World Council of Churches.

An informed, straight-thinking public is the only hope of democracy. The strength of Christendom lies in individuals similarly oriented. In the light of these truths it is well to consider carefully some pertinent questions and answers about the World Council of Churches prepared by the General Secretariat, Geneva, Switzerland, for the conference at Toronto in July of 1950 in order to understand what it is and what it plans to do and how to accomplish that purpose.

WHAT IS THE WORLD COUNCIL OF CHURCHES?

It is, according to the Constitution, "a fellowship of Churches which accept Our Lord Jesus Christ as God and Saviour." The 156 churches from all parts of the world and from all major Christian confessions except Roman Catholicism, which have joined it, have thus expressed their desire "to stay together" in order to come to know one another, to labor together in common tasks, to render common witness and to prepare the way for a fuller manifestation of Christian unity. They have done so because they believe that, even though they cannot yet arrive at full unity in faith and order, they should manifest such unity as is already a reality among them. The World Council is, therefore, in no sense an aim in itself. It is wholly an instrument which seeks to serve the churches in the performing of tasks which the churches desire to accomplish together. And the nature of its activities depends altogether on the decisions which are taken by the official representatives of the churches in its Assembly or Central Committee.

WHAT IS THE SIGNIFICANCE OF ITS BASIS?

The basis of the World Council of Churches which accept Our Lord Jesus Christ as God and Saviour is not a "confession" in the sense that it seeks to express the faith of the participating churches in its fullness. It is rather a statement concerning the starting point for the conversation between the churches in the Council and concerning the indispensable foundation of their co-operation. Only such churches are eligible for World Council membership as express agreement with the basis. The World Council has neither the authority nor the competence to question the doctrinal position of the churches, so that it remains the responsibility of each church to decide whether it will co-operate on this basis. Some churches have found it impossible to accept this basis. The delegates represented at the Assembly, however, said unanimously that the basis is adequate for the present purposes of the World Council, that any churches that may desire change in the basis should present their desires in writing to the Central Committee for study and report to the next Assembly; and that the Central Committee be instructed that no proposed change could be considered which compromised on the Christological affirmation of the present basis.

IS THE WORLD COUNCIL DOMINATED
BY A PARTICULAR THEOLOGY?

Within the constituency of the World Council all the confessional theologies of the participating Church are represented. And to these must be added the different theological trends which cut across denominational lines. There is, therefore, no "World Council theology." Nor can any particular theological school gain control of the Council. The agreed statements which the Council issues, such as the reports of the Assembly or of study conferences, represent the outcome of a process of confrontation of very diverse convictions. Only such common statements, not statements of individuals, are to be taken as reflecting not only the area of agreement, but also the relevant points of disagreement which require further discussion. The World Council stands for a frank and searching conversation about the truth of God in the hope that, as the Assembly put it, "the churches may be bound closer to Christ and therefore closer to one another."

HAS THE WORLD COUNCIL RELATIONSHIPS WITH THE ROMAN CATHOLIC CHURCH?

The authorities of the Roman Catholic Church have stated repeatedly that their church cannot enter into a Council of Churches. The recent Vatican instructions reaffirm that attitude. The Roman Catholic Church was, therefore, not invited to send official delegates to the Amsterdam Assembly. In view of the interest shown by certain Roman Catholic circles, some unofficial observers of that church were invited to attend the Assembly, but none of these came because the Vatican forbade it.

Thus the World Council has no relationships with the Vatican. On the other hand, in fields of practical activity such as the work among refugees, Departments of the Council have had occasion to work with Roman Catholic bodies. And Roman Catholic theologians have sometimes been asked to contribute to specific studies undertaken by World Council Departments.

In matters of religious liberty the World Council has more

than once taken a firm stand against the infringements of
religious liberties in countries in which the Roman Catholic
Church has a dominant position.

IS THE WORLD COUNCIL CONCERNED
WITH POLITICS?

The World Council is completely independent of governmental or political bodies or parties. Within its far-flung
constituency very many different convictions and attitudes
with regard to current social and political problems may be
found. The World Council does not identify itself with any
national, political or social stand. But that does not mean
that the World Council is not concerned with the life of the
nations and with society. One of the traditions which it repre-
sents is that of the "Life and Work" movement which has
always stood for the proclamation of the Christian witness in
relation to social, national and international life. And the
Council considers it its duty to impress the common mind of
the churches about the great spiritual and moral issues which
have to be faced in our time. Through the Commission of
the Churches on International Affairs (under the common
auspices of the World Council of Churches and the International Missionary Council), it seeks in particular to express
the demands of the Christian conscience as to international
issues. Thus it has taken a firm stand on such questions as
human rights, religious liberty, the refugee problem, treatment
of war criminals, atomic warfare.

IS THE WORLD COUNCIL AN ATTEMPT
TO CREATE A SUPERCHURCH?

The World Council is in no sense an administrative or ecclesiastical body which exerts authority over the churches.

Its constitution explicitly forbids it to legislate for the churches. And it can take action on behalf of constituent churches only in such matters as one or more of them may commit to it. In order to make this point as clear as possible, the Assembly at Amsterdam adopted a statement to the effect that "the Council is far from desiring to usurp any of the functions which already belong to its constituent churches, or to control them, or to legislate for them." It is, therefore, most misleading to describe the Council as "the World Church," for the phrase suggests a type of integration and unity that does not exist in the World Council. The Council is simply a servant of the churches which helps them to enter into living contact with one another and to do the things which they want to do together.

IS THE WORLD COUNCIL DOMINATED BY ANY GROUP OF CHURCHES?

The membership of the World Council is made up of churches of many different confessions and many different structures. Some of the oldest and some of the youngest churches participate in its life. There are churches which have an official relation with the state and far more which have no connection with any government. (Four fifths of the membership of the Central Committee represent the last named.) All the major Christian confessions (except the Roman Catholic) are represented. Thus each confessional group finds itself a minority in the World Council. No group of churches can dominate the life of the body as a whole.

The same is true with regard to nationalities. The Central Committee has members of 30 nations, the Executive Committee of 9 nations and the World Council staff of 14 nations. In such a situation it is out of the question that any particular nationality could succeed in having its own way regardless of the wishes of others. The Council seeks precisely to manifest the fullness and riches of the fellowship in Christ of all nationalities.

IS THE WORLD COUNCIL CONCERNED WITH THE LAITY?

The World Council is an ecclesiastical body in the sense that it is an official organ of the participating churches. But that does not mean that it is a body of and for "ecclesiastics." There are 15 laymen on its Central Committee and 4 on its Executive Committee. And the Council is specially active in helping to mobilize the lay forces in the churches. One of the Committees of the Amsterdam Assembly dealt with "The Significance of the Laity in the Church." And the Ecumenical Institute (near Geneva) makes it its main business to help laymen in the different professions to witness in their special lines to the relevance of the Gospel for society. The Assembly decided that in the coming years a number of area conferences for the laity should be organized for the purpose of enlisting the full lay power of the Church for its task in the world. Many laymen are active in the various World Council Committees, notably in the Study Department, the Ecumenical Institute and the Commission of the Churches on International Affairs (a common Committee with the International Missionary Council).

IS THE WORLD COUNCIL CONCERNED WITH THE EVANGELISTIC TASK OF THE CHURCH?

Evangelism was one of the main subjects discussed. The Assembly felt so strongly that Evangelism is the first and foremost task of the churches that it set up a special World Council Secretariat for Evangelism, so that the churches may learn from one another and help one another in this all important field.

Concern of the World Council with world evangelism finds clear expression also in the fact that it has entered into association with the International Missionary Council, the body formed by the Missionary Councils in the West and the National Christian Councils in Asia, Africa and elsewhere. The close collaboration between the World Council of Churches and the International Missionary Council is a visible manifestation of the common conviction that the missionary movement is an essential part of the ecumenical movement in its widest sense.

Many churches which have grown up as a result of modern missions are members of the Council and bring their evangelistic concern into the common life of the movement.

WHAT IS THE ATTITUDE OF THE WORLD COUNCIL TOWARD CHURCH UNITY?

The World Council does not unite churches in the sense that it takes steps to effect their union in faith and order. Each church in the Council remains wholly free in its decisions concerning the nature of its relations with other churches. The Council, notably through its commission on Faith and Order, helps the churches to study the issues of church unity. Thus it seeks to remove misunderstandings and to promote a frank facing of existing differences. At the same time, by bringing the churches into living contact with one another, through its conferences, courses and interchurch activities, it seeks to foster that sense of ecumenical solidarity and fellowship which is the indispensable basis for any advance toward Christian unity. Within the constituency of the Council many different conceptions of church unity are represented. The Council cannot identify itself with any particular conception, because its *raison d'être* is precisely to serve as a meeting place where these various convictions are confronted with one another. The Council has, however, gone on record as disavowing "any thought of becoming a single unified church structure independent of the churches" or "a structure dominated by a centralized administrative authority." The Council is only an instrument of the churches which helps to prepare the way for unity.

ORGANIZATION OF THE WORLD COUNCIL OF CHURCHES

The task of the General Secretariat (composed of one General Secretary and five Associate General Secretaries, several of whom are at the same time heads of departments) is to carry out the policies decided on by the Assembly or the Central Committee, to co-ordinate the activities of the departments and secretariats, to maintain relationships through correspondence and visitation with the constituent churches and to prepare the meetings of the Central Committee and the Assembly.

The function of the Commission on Faith and Order is to make a thorough study of such differences in the faith and the order of the churches as are obstacles to their full unity and to find possible ways to overcome these differences. This commission seeks also to hold the challenge of unity before the churches and to inform them periodically about developments relating to union.

The Study Department initiates and promotes ecumenical study projects among the member churches. It carries special responsibility in preparing for World Council Assemblies. Its present program includes three world-wide inquiries: "The Bible and the Church's Message to the World"; "The Evangelization of Men in Modern Mass Society"; "Christian

Action in Society" (subdivided into "A Responsible Society" and "The Meaning of Work").

The Department of Interchurch Aid and Service to Refugees seeks to find help for the most vital needs of the churches in Europe. It studies the needs of the European churches, draws up programs for assistance and co-ordinates the giving. It has developed a health program for church leaders and a scholarship program for theological students. Its service to refugees includes ministering to their spiritual needs, as well as assistance in resettlement.

The Youth Department seeks to help the churches and in particular their youth organizations in giving to their young people a sense of participation in and responsibility for the ecumenical movement. It promotes solidarity among church youth organizations and provides opportunities for personal ecumenical contacts.

The Department of Finance and Business is responsible for accounting, drawing up budgets, raising contributions from the churches, supervising the expenditure of the departments, transmitting interchurch-aid funds and in general for all matters concerning the financing of World Council activities.

The Ecumenical Institute, located near Geneva, holds training courses for ministers, theological students, youth leaders and church workers in order to give them direct ecumenical experience and education. It helps laymen in various professions and occupations to arrive at a clear understanding of the specific Christian vocation in their particular sector of modern secular society. It is also the co-ordinating center of the various movements and institutes for lay training and lay activities.

The Secretariat for Evangelism was set up in order to stimulate and assist the churches in meeting more adequately their responsibilities for the proclamation of the Gospel of

Christ to all men everywhere in all their individual and social relationships. It acts as a clearinghouse for information on new forms and methods of evangelism. In this it collaborates closely with the International Missionary Council.

There is a Commission on the Life and Work of Women in the Church. Its functions are to stimulate study and action in the churches with regard to the place of women in church life, to encourage an ecumenical outlook in the women's organizations and to promote the sharing of experiences among them.

Scholars from many churches and countries are collaborating in the task of producing two volumes; one dealing with ecumenical history up to the year 1910, another describing the development from 1910 to 1948. This work is under the Director of the Commission on the History of the Ecumenical Movement.

The *Ecumenical Review* is the official organ of the Council. It appears quarterly under the direction of an editorial board with members of different churches and nations. Within its pages a conversation among the churches on all questions of common concern is pursued. It provides its readers at the same time with a continuous record of the main developments within the life of the ecumenical movement.

There is an Ecumenical Press Service, under the joint auspices of seven international Christian bodies. It appears weekly in three languages and provides information about the life of the churches and the ecumenical movement. Its news items are widely used in the religious press, and also in the secular press of some countries. World Council press officers in Geneva and New York are in constant touch with the press of many nations.

Under the joint auspices of the World Council of Churches and the International Missionary Council the Commission on International Affairs serves the churches as a source of stimulus and knowledge in their approach to international problems, as a medium of common counsel and action, and as their organ in dealing with world issues. This Commission has a consultative status with the United Nations.

It is significant that the message of the First Assembly of the World Council of Churches adopted the following resolution:

Here at Amsterdam we have committed ourselves afresh to Him and have covenanted with one another in constituting the World Council of Churches. We intend to stay together. We call upon Christian congregations everywhere to endorse and fulfill this covenant in their relations one with another.

It is one thing to form a World Council and another to achieve real fellowship and co-operation among local churches of various denominations. This was recognized by the Amsterdam Conference, which frankly said:

Our coming together to form a World Council will be in vain unless Christians and Christian congregations everywhere commit themselves to the Lord of the Church in a new effort to seek together, where we live, to be His witnesses and servants among their neighbors.

Everyone in the Protestant Church, minister and layman, should keep himself informed about this world-wide movement. Helpful material is available at the World Council of Churches, 297 Fourth Avenue, New York City, for those who really want to know about this most important event in centuries. Do you know what the World Council is doing? Do you belong to the continuing reformation that humbly acknowledges man's disorder and is gravely concerned to know what is God's design?

I am a Protestant who is hopeful that churches throughout the world, thus united in the spirit and purpose of Christ, may overcome the totalitarian way of life, Statism, Fascism or Communism. The democratic way will not, however, overcome the totalitarian way until and unless the democracies somehow crusade under the banner of the Church. How can we defeat the destructive dynamics of Fascism and Communism unless we employ the constructive dynamics of the Christian Spirit and are "baptized with the Spirit and with fire"?

William Penn said, "Men must be governed by God or they will be ruled by tyrants." The world today, suffering under tyranny, is eloquent witness to the truth of his utterance.

9

THE CHURCH OF THE FUTURE

THE Protestant Reformation of the sixteenth century, we have seen, was not an isolated event that occurred once and for all in history; neither was it just a protest against the corruption of the Roman Church of that day. The Reformation was the beginning of a new movement in religion based not on an ignoble submission to self-constituted authority, but on the voluntary witness of man, who has the ability to answer for himself directly to God and acknowledges the authority of Christ as the head of the Church and seeks to know and do his will. Wrote John Locke:

A Church I take to be a voluntary society of men joining themselves of their own accord in order to exercise the public worshipping of God in such manner as they judge acceptable to Him, and effectual to the salvation of their souls. . . . I say it is a free and voluntary society. Nobody is born a member of any church.

Yet an honest evaluation of the Protestant Church reveals its weakness as well as its strength. Primarily because of the emphasis the Protestants place on sectarianism, which grew out of a false use of the Bible as an authority for the establishment of the various Protestant churches, the Roman Catholic Church is presented with the opportunity to point to the more than 250 denominational "Churches," or "splinters" as the Catholics term them, and say with scorn: "See how divided you are! How can you claim to be ecumenical?"

My good Catholic friend, Edward J. Donnellan, of Chicago, learning that I was writing this book, asked me to read a current book by Thomas McDermott entitled *Certainly, I'm a Catholic!* I read it with careful interest. It is written by an educated American, who states the case for Catholicism as "the only acceptable way of life for a reasonable man." In a rather unusual approach to the subject Mr. McDermott reveals why a young Catholic layman, liking a "good time," possessing the normal desires of his age and position, remains a Catholic. McDermott presents Catholicism as a way of life and a system of thought. I have obtained the author's permission to quote three paragraphs from his last chapter, "Another Question," pages 149 and 150.

We, the people of today, fear tomorrow. We have cause to fear because a civilization is ending, and a new one, or the lack of one, is forming. What system of thought and way of life holds out the best hope for a peaceful and secure future? Protestantism, I reluctantly conclude, has long since disqualified itself by failing to develop a consistent and useful system of thought and way of life. It has no united and effective philosophy of social justice, as is to be found in the papal encyclicals, but merely echoes the voices of the economic regime currently in power. Protestants, lay and clerical, are as sincerely interested as Catholics in securing justice for all men, and are arduously striving for it; but they are like a lost motorist without a map, following one road and then another, turning a corner here and doubling back there.

The same pathetic situation is true of Protestantism and international peace and order. The Protestants of every nation work as hard for peace as do Catholics, but for what kind of peace—what are to be its bases? its motives? and its sanctions? Even if Protestantism offers specific and sound answers to these questions, it has no foundations with which to support them, at least none not subject to change. And the great tragedy of Protestantism—it has no unity with which to make its system of thought and way of life an adamant weapon against the forces of tyranny and the minions of evil. If the Protestant groups cannot agree on what man is and why he is on earth, they cannot be unified on the rights and duties of labor and capital or the requisites for a lasting and prosperous peace.

Protestantism, which began in the sixteenth century, has in the course of the three hundred ensuing years, proved itself to be a failure. The original Protestant religion of Martin Luther has splintered into some three hundred fragments, each different from and opposed to all the others, the degree ranging from incidental to essential and from minor to bitter hostility. The thought and life of Protestantism have dominated the political and the economic history of the Western world. Today, that thought and that life are being rejected by the peoples of the Western world, and they are turning either to communism or to Catholicism, or to secularism. Protestantism has indeed become a voice speaking in the wilderness of its own making and echoing back from unhearing ears. It exists today principally to protest against the Catholic system of thought and way of life. If Protestantism contained a true and sound answer to chaos, it would today be a unified expression of its founding and not a historical failure.

There are many ways of dealing with this blistering indictment. One is the way of blind prejudice which says, "That is what one would expect of a Catholic." There is nothing to be gained when a Protestant condemns a Roman Catholic, who may be as honest as he in seeking the will of God in his own life; or when a Roman Catholic does the same thing to a Protestant who is equally earnest and sincere in his religious devotion. The Irishmen's paradoxical, whimsical and disturbing remark is worth recalling: "If we were only heathens, perhaps we could be able to live together as Christians." We must face the fact, however, that union with the Church of Rome is not possible without complete submission to the Pope, because the Roman Church maintains that its particular hierarchy is "the only true Church," and is alone of divine institution. Therefore, relationship on any reciprocal basis is blocked.

Another way is by enumerating the weaknesses of the Roman Catholic Church. They are many. Chief among these, as we have noted, is the autocratic, dictatorial and totalitarian system of the Roman Catholic Church which tends to stifle man's freedom to find God and worship and serve Him. Primarily because of this fact many thoughtful Roman Catholics are leaving that Church. One of the most startling reports is an article which is part one of a study of Roman Catholic losses throughout the world to the American Episcopal Church during the last ten years, 1940-1950.

In a statement in *Time* (January 9, 1950) the Archbishop of York commented on the "continuous stream of those who are leaving Rome and looking elsewhere for their spiritual home." This comment is confirmed by an article entitled "Conversions from Roman Catholicism" in the *Living Church,* a weekly record of the news, the work and the thoughts of the Episcopal Church:

We have felt that the clergy and laity of our Church were sometimes disturbed by the commonly asserted claim that the Church of Rome is making great inroads upon not only our membership, but upon the membership of all non-Roman communions and denominations, and is seeking thereby to create an attitude of defeatism and submission among the non-Roman Christian world.

We may therefore state, with great leaning to the conservative side, that in the past 10 years (1940-1950) the American Episcopal Church has formally received at the hands of its bishops 26,242 persons from the Roman Communion into the Anglican Communion.

In addition to the laity, there have been 14 priests received into active pastoral relationship with the dioceses of this Church within the past 10 years. Many of the bishops stated, in their generous correspondence, that they had many Roman priests applying to them for admission into Anglican obedience, but that, because of the difficulties involved in checking their records under Roman authority, their applications were not acted upon.

The question naturally arises, how many have gone out from the Episcopal to the Roman Catholic Church? To this the authors of the article reply in their last paragraph:

We have no way of ascertaining the number who have left the Episcopal Church to journey in the opposite direction. From an informal survey among rectors of sizable parishes in the vicinity of New York, the number reported would seem to indicate that we gain ten for each one lost.

These figures are confirmed by a partial check with clergymen of other denominations. For example, I can report as minister of the Bryn Mawr Community Church in Chicago that out of the over 2,300 persons received into membership in the past eight years, 143 who were confirmed adult Roman Catholics were received into our membership without proselyting efforts. During that same period, 13 members of the Bryn Mawr Community Church have become members of the Roman Catholic Church.

The fairest and most profitable way of answering Mr. McDermott's indictment is for us to face the weaknesses of the Protestant churches and seek to correct them. I am indebted to Dr. James R. Killian, Jr., President of Massachusetts Institute of Technology, for an apt story. A golfer hit his ball on the fairway and it finally came to rest on an anthill. He took his #7 club, addressed the ball and took a mighty swing, knocking away one fourth of the anthill, killing all the ants in that section of the hill but never touching the ball. He took another stance and a mightier swing, with the result that he knocked down another fourth of the anthill, killing all the ants in that section too but again never touching the ball. This was repeated a third time with the same result. As he was preparing to take his fourth swing the ants in the remaining fourth of the hill got together and hastily proclaimed this wise decision to one another: "If we are going to survive, we must get on the ball."

Even though the indictment by Thomas McDermott is biased and therefore only partially true, nevertheless it has truth enough in it to cause us to pause and examine with care our Protestant faith and resolve to "get on the ball." We would do well to face frankly the charges leveled against us by this layman of the Roman Church, honestly study our weaknesses and earnestly endeavor to learn the why of them and how we may correct our faults so we may become an increasingly strong and potent religious force in America and the world.

For one thing we will discover that the present denominational system of churches is both insincere and ineffective. The claim that each denomination has some great and unique truth, which makes it distinctive and marks it off from others, is often conveniently forgotten at both the ordination of ministers and the reception of new members. This has led many thoughtful persons to conclude that the distinctive features claimed by this or that particular denomination no longer exist or that they are unimportant.

What then is needed? What are the signs of hope in this confused and confusing age? What about the Protestant Church of the future? Do we need another Reformation? These are questions that cannot be easily silenced.

We face a divided world, where secularism is the dominant force, and to a large extent is found to pervade the thought and action of the Protestant churches. We face a world in revolution, with Communism embraced by millions as their faith: a faith founded on a material basis, which has great appeal to the large number of people of the world, the "have-nots." Burdened by a name which, because it is misunderstood is a liability rather than an asset, the Protestant Church faces an uncertain future. What can it do in "the mad, mad world" in which we live, that the light of God's truth may shine?

There is one heartening sign, and it is this: there is an increasing realization that impotent sectarianism is not the answer. The only hope for our effete civilization is a religion of truth and power. Another thing we know, beyond any doubt, is that there can be no revival of moral integrity without a vital religion. Therefore, the Church of the future must be effective.

A united strategy is required in order to attain this worthy goal. This calls for the ablest leadership from every church planning and working together so that a united spiritual impact may be made on our world for the good of all, not so much for the sake of the churches as for the sake of the people. This co-operation and unification must be practiced by the churches in a community in order that through a unity of concentrated action a helpful influence may be made by the united church upon our misguided and chaotic world.

What shall we call the Church of the future? Will it be "Apostolic," "Community," "United," "Catholic," "Christian" or "Ecumenical"? Each name has merit and each has some weakness. Perhaps "Ecumenical" is the best. Yet it is a cumbersome word, difficult for the ordinary mind of man to readily understand.

What does *catholic* really mean? It is a noble word. We ought not to abandon it to a single branch of the Church of Christ, and that to the least truly Catholic. We ought never to speak of the Roman Church as "the Catholic Church," never to use the word "Roman Catholic" as meaning the ecumenical church. The word meant originally, and should now be used as meaning, "the Church taken as a whole," the comprehensive Church, the whole body of believers in Christ, the Church that includes all the branches and divisions of Christianity. To believe in the Catholic Church is to deny all exclusive pretensions in one particular little denomination. It is to declare one's faith in one's own part of the Church only insofar as that part is trying to realize the name which truly connotes the idea of the great comprehensive body of Christ.

Paul was filled with the true Catholic spirit when he prayed for his friends and for all Christians that they might come to know "with all the saints . . . what is the length and depth and height and breadth of the religion of Christ." To believe in the true Catholic Church is to believe in a comprehensive, inclusive Church, which takes in and rejoices over the infinite diversity of thought and feeling in its fellowship, counting the Church richer for all its variety. It means that we take as our own all that is true and good in any part of the Christian Church, since "all things are ours, and we are Christ's and Christ is God's." That is why, in its truest sense, "the Communion of Saints" means also that we gladly claim fellowship with a wider circle than that circumscribed by the bounds of any particular church. We claim fellowship with all true lovers of God and servants of man who are actuated by the Spirit of Christ.

Professor Latourette, of Yale University, contends that someday the scandal of division will be overcome because all of us will have had the good sense and Christian grace to go beyond our present sectarianism to the basic Christianity of personal and group commitment to one Lord and Saviour. There is a possibility of this being achieved by the Protestant churches.

How will it be accomplished? For one thing, by the intelligent and consecrated laymen in the churches. Elton Trueblood in his recent book, *Signs of Hope,* points to the emergence of a lay religion as a sign of great promise. It is finding expression at the grass roots in the local churches and in all the city, state, national and world movements, both denominational and interdenominational. Here is the beginning of a trend of spiritual power and unlimited promise. It will also come through the awakened clergy who go back to Jesus and take his word and way of life in earnest.

Again, if a new world is to be built by Christian principles, it will be built only by men and women who have learned to hold those principles constantly before them. Dr. Bail Matthews is reported to have asked Sir Alfred Zimmern, "What in your opinion is the chief obstacle between us and an enduring peace?" Without hesitation Sir Alfred replied, "The small-scale individual." So it is with the Church and the Christian. We dare not be small-scale Christians today. We must keep the mighty perspective of God ever before our eyes.

The Church of the future must be interested also in man as man. The Protestant Church has tended to be interested primarily in the middle and upper classes. The Protestant Church of the future dare not continue to be a class Church! It must be interested in all men. It must be an inclusive Church, including not only all people of different denominational backgrounds but all kinds and conditions of men.

Nothing would make me happier than to be ordained by every Church in Christendom, by Bishop, Presbytery, or any other authority; but I should insist, in my heart at least, on having the taxi-driver, the washer-woman, the ditch-digger, the flapper with her painted fingernails, the baker, and, not least of all, the chubby hand of a little child laid upon my head giving me their human blessing. Then, perhaps, I might be a priest of the human soul, healing its hurts, uttering its deepest desires, answering even its unasked questions, and also a prophet of the Love of God, which is all that matters.[1]

The position in which Jesus placed his Church was that of "a city that is set on a hill." It would compel the attention of the world. This must start at the local level. Protestantism has too often been weak at its base, namely, the local church. It is heartening to note a new sense of mission and a searching for the true function of the local church on the part of individual churches. It isn't enough to deal in clichés, such as "let the Church be the Church," unless we understand what Archbishop Temple had in mind when he said that the primary concern of the Church is to remind men that if they neglect God they cannot make a success of life, and it is the business of the Church to help man find God and his available resources. The one primary concern of the Church is religion, the development of persons as children of God. This requires three great qualities: intelligent concern, glad loyalty and high adventure.

Recently there has been an earnest "taking of stock" and evaluation through surveys by churches. For example, the First Congregational Church at Madison, Wisconsin, made a self-analysis of its religious enterprise for the year 1949, and today it has in its hands a 200-page "Report and Recommendations of the General Survey Committee." It is now moving ahead with an immediate ten-point program of reform and improvement to better the needs of its members, the city of Madison and the world. The motive of this study was not to make the Church more efficient so much as to make it more effective.

The Church of Christ need not be one in organization, but

---

[1] Joseph Fort Newton, *The River of Years* (Philadelphia, J. B. Lippincott Company, 1946), p. 233. Reprinted by permission of the publishers.

it must be one in spirit and united in a common effort to make Christ regnant in all of life. Our first duty as Christians is to evidence to the world our unity in Christ as something far greater than our difference in interpretation. If we cannot heal our divisions we can at least face the pagan philosophy and the evils of this world with a united strength, agreeing to differ and resolving to serve a common Lord and Master. We need to hear the Church of the future lift up her voice like a trumpet and proclaim that the life of a man, made in the image of God, is worth more than that of a sheep.

THE PREACHING FUNCTION

A revitalized Church is an essential in tomorrow's world. To be specific it means that greater emphasis will be placed on the true preaching function of the Church. As John Orman says in *Honest Religion*:

The churches are troubled but it is about their numbers, their finances, their enterprises, and not about what alone matters gravely, their message and the employment of it in their fellowship.

So much has been written about preaching that only two brief suggestions need be made. First, preachers should deal with great themes that really matter, with the roots of religions: God, man, Christ, the Cross, the Kingdom of God, sin, salvation and human destiny. The great affirmatives of the Gospel clamor for expression. Like St. Paul, every preacher should exclaim: "Woe is unto me, if I preach not the gospel!"

Second, the Beecher Lectures on Preaching given at Yale by the great preachers of the English-speaking world should be read and studied by every preacher. Phillips Brooks defined preaching as "the transmission of truth through personality." Dr. Henry Sloane Coffin added to this classic definition, "Preaching is the transmission of truth through personality *to a person.*" It is making truth portable to human understanding and need. It considers not only the subject of preaching but also gives consideration to the object of preaching.

THE TEACHING FUNCTION

The church school must include not only children but all the adult members of the Church. We need to stress *content, worship* and *projects,* and in that order. The ministers and directors of religious education are increasingly recognizing two needs: One, *content,* the knowledge of the Bible and church history and the basic ideas on which the Church is founded; Two, *adult religious education.* This last is being provided through parents' classes, study groups and instruction to those who are to be received into the fellowship of the Church. For example, the Madison Avenue Presbyterian Church in New York City, under Dr. George A. Buttrick's able leadership, has successfully conducted an Adult Lenten School. Enrollment is limited to 600 persons and the applications each year exceed that number. Bryn Mawr Community Church of Chicago has conducted the second Annual Lenten School for Adults. Last year the enrollment was 209. This year it was 251. It is heartening that there is a desire and willingness of busy adults to give one full evening of three hours each week throughout Lent to a study concerning beliefs that matter in connection with their religious faith. It is obvious that adult education for parents and older people in the home must have knowledge of the Christian faith in order to have the church school effective.

THE HEALING FUNCTION

The Protestant Church must exercise its healing function, for it is the custodian of a gospel designed to meet the deepest needs of humanity. Men are harassed by anxiety and fears, oppressed by a sense of frustration and futility, in desperate need of deliverance from self-centeredness and conflicting desire, bewildered by the predicament of modern life. Never were so many restless, discontented and tense people everywhere seeking for the good news about life—and finding a dead-end street. To relax is not enough, and yet it is necessary to learn how to relax as a means to healthy living. A Negro mammy who was asked the secret of her poise and peace, answered "When I works, I works hard. When I sets I sets loose."

We grant that the Roman Catholic Church confessional has great value if used aright, but it has too often been abused. The Protestant Church has recently realized that it is part of its ministry to "heal the broken-hearted" and minister to the perplexed and confused. Marcus Dods at the near end of his life said that if he could have his ministry over again he would preach oftener on the comfort of God.

Marked attention has been given, in recent years, both in seminaries and in the local parish, to pastoral work and pastoral counseling. After thirty glorious years in the ministry I have condensed my ideas on counseling to four basic principles.

First: Be a sympathetic listener. There is great value in catharsis, that is, a purging, the "spilling" of what is on one's mind and soul.

Second: It is difficult to do good by advice without the danger of doing harm.

Third: It is not possible to help those who do not have the desire and the ability to help themselves.

Fourth: Help those whom you counsel to find the resources in their religious faith through prayer, meditation, reading the Bible and devotional literature and the forgetting of self in serving others.

Much helpful work is being done in the healing ministry by Doctors John Sutherland Bonnell, pastor of the Fifth Avenue Presbyterian Church, New York City; James William Fifield, pastor of the First Congregational Church, Los Angeles; Lloyd Ellis Foster, pastor of Old First Presbyterian Church, Newark, New Jersey; James Gordon Gilkey, pastor of the South Congregational Church, Springfield, Massachusetts; Norman Vincent Peale, pastor of the Marble Collegiate Reformed Church, New York City; Luther E. Stein, pastor of the First Presbyterian Church, Oak Park, Illinois, and Harry Emerson Fosdick, pastor emeritus of the Riverside Church, New York City, whose *On Being a Real Person* is a classic on understanding and helping oneself. All these have contributed each in his own way to the development of a healing ministry.

THE PROPHETIC MINISTRY

We have many "live wires" in the Protestant churches today but few prophets and seers. There are many things in the world that make for the lack of even the opportunity for quality of life and abundant living on the part of many. One of these is war.

The outspoken hatred of war is old, but never before has there been such a rising tide of revulsion against it as in our day. More and more thoughtful Christians are convinced that war is not in the program of God. Rather it is the problem of God and of men of good will and righteousness.

Peace cannot be improvised. We are naturally tempted to

an oversimplified or nonpolitical way of gaining peace. We have been taught that it takes good men to make a good world. That is true, but we must also see that our political and economic setup, which is now based on competing national sovereignties, divides a world. We must have a uniting of the nations if we are to deal successfully with this problem of war which is the sum total of all sin, both individual and collective. It is not enough for the Church to create good men; it must create the creators of a new social order which will effect an adequate political and economic structure that will come to grips with this world-wide problem. If we do not do both—create good men and create a worthy structure—we shall suffer one debacle after another. After every war we "fasten upon ourselves the sins of our beaten enemies." Soon, all too soon, we will be hopelessly impotent and lost. It is later than we think!

Herman Hagedorn says in his poem, "The Bomb That Fell on America":

"There is power in the human soul," said the Lord,
"When you break through and set it free.
  Like the power of the atom.
  More powerful than the atom,
  It can control the atom,
  The only thing in the world that can.
  I told you that the atom is the greatest force in the world,
        save one.
  That one is the human soul.
"But," said the Lord—and the stars in the sky seemed to
        stand still and listen—
"The power must be released, as the atom-breakers released
        the power of the atom.
  They had to get past the electrons to get at the energy
        packed in the nucleus.
  And I have to get past a deal of ego to release the power
        that is packed in the soul of man.

I keep shooting My rays toward the nucleus,
And the charged field keeps fending them off.
But now and then one gets by,
The nucleus is split, the power is released, and things begin
    to happen on a scale that makes men gasp and talk
    about miracles.
But it isn't a miracle.
It's just the soul of man coming to its own.
It's just the soul of man freed at last to be itself."

The Lord He looked at me and His eyes pierced like hot
    wires.
"Perhaps," He said, "there's something in you and numerous
    others that will have to be cracked open, if a
    hundred and thirty-five million people are going
    to grow up overnight.
"Something in you," said the Lord, "something, perhaps, in
    you."

That was a joke, and I laughed. But the Lord wasn't
    laughing.[2]

I am indebted to my brother, Dr. Chester Ezekiel Jenney, for the following pertinent illustration: Some years ago when Woodrow Wilson was President, at an Old Home Day gathering in Cornish, New Hampshire, Percy MacKay gave one of his own dramatizations at the afternoon session. President Wilson was in attendance. World War I was being fought on the soil of France. The background of this dramatic bit of reading was the Revolutionary War. The scene was Valley Forge, a terrible winter of hunger and suffering for Washington's ragged and hungry army. A soldier from northern New York deserted that army. He had had enough. He started home. As he journeyed, the wilderness through which he passed became vocal with a voice. It was the voice

---

[2] Herman Hagedorn, "The Bomb That Fell on America," in Kirby Page's *Living Joyfully* (New York and Toronto, Rinehart & Company, 1950), p. 77. Reprinted by permission.

of his innermost soul. Over and over the message came. "You are the one in whom liberty is lost. You are the one in whom liberty is saved." This soldier turned around, went back to Valley Forge, rejoined his company, endured the suffering and died at Yorktown. We are in the wilderness. The drouth of war is on. For weal or woe, as future years unfold, the voice we hear is the voice, "In me liberty is lost. In me liberty is saved." So it is that: In me peace is won!

THE FUNCTION OF WITNESSING

The intelligently concerned ministers and laymen of the Protestant Church have come to realize that the Church in the Greek sense of the word is the *ecclesia,* originally meaning "the called out." Although we ought not in seriousness to expect an infallible church out of fallible people, nevertheless the acid test of the Church is the Christian. Many programs like the New Life Movement of the Presbyterian Church, U. S. A., have been of value in increasing church membership and in raising money. By many it is hoped that also a deeper spiritual note might be the true emphasis.

Statistics of church membership, attendance and finances do not tell the whole story. It is possible for the Church to have an outward appearance of health and yet not know inwardly the reason why it exists. It is one thing to maintain an organization and another to hold on to a living faith in Jesus Christ. The most efficiently organized and enthusiastically attended Church may readily be out of touch with Christ's purpose and with the life around it, and without any effective spiritual influence on the lives of men within it.

The effective Church of the future will come not so much through organization, although that is necessary, as by the spirit of Christ.

It is the purpose of Jesus Christ to unify the Church. . . .
The unity of Christendom is not a luxury but a necessity. . . .
Division is the Achilles' heel of the Christian enterprise. . . .
A split Church can present only a split Christ.

Thus Bishop Brent, a pioneer of the ecumenical church, put it
in vivid language and with penetrating insight, as quoted in a
recent book about his life and saying, *Things That Matter*.

Church Unity will come after Christian Unity. It would
not be gain to aim at oneness as an end in itself. Mere oneness
would be a sort of saccharine monotony in which differences
would not have been reconciled but rather smothered and
hidden under a thick coat of sentimentality. Unity, as I
understand it, will come as the result of a wholehearted
devotion to a common center, a common vision, and a common
purpose. We do not seek for unity in order to come to Christ,
but in coming to Christ we are thereby committed to unity
according to His mind, and if we fail to find unity we have
missed the way.[3]

There are those who believe that a new Protestantism is
emerging from anarchic sectarianism as the true Ecumenical
Church of Christ. Only such a Church can provide the religious resources needed to gather up the fragments of a
shattered civilization and build a new earth in which righteousness dwells. This "age of the Spirit" will come through
faith, prayer and dedicated living. A new age is here if we
are prepared to receive it. Like the pearl of great price it will
cost all we have—all we have is always the price of the best.
The new age, in which the Spirit of God will reign, will be
worth this cost.

Dr. G. Bromley Oxnam ends his recently published book,
On This Rock, with the following:

---

[3] *Things That Matter: The Best of the Writings of Bishop Brent* (New
York, Harper & Brothers, 1949), pp. 39, 42. Reprinted by permission of the
publishers.

Repentance and dedication are essential. There must be a new consecration upon the part of every Christian. Each member must kneel at the altar of his own church and there in prayer, devotion, and worship come to a deepened experience of Christ. There must be a plea for forgiveness for all the practices that root in pride and the love of power; penitence for the divisive spirit that has refused to accept new truth. The churches themselves must ask God to forgive them. There has been far too much of pride or loyalty to nation or class, far too much of the desire to maintain vested interest. From all of this we must be cleansed.

The idea of the united Church is abroad. Its time has come. It is an idea of power; it is present in the thinking of youth. Perhaps the surest way to progress is to unite the great families of similar tradition first. But we need not wait upon that. When a Church is ready, let it take decision in its own way, appoint plenipotentiaries to sit in conference with representatives of other communions until the spirit moves. Whatever may be the method eventually used, certain it is that upon the confession of Peter, the united Church will be built and someday not alone in the Vermont village but everywhere we may receive the blessings of the united Church if we are but Christian enough, persistent enough, intelligent enough.[4]

A Church that makes so little difference it can be ignored by the world is a Church whose light is dim. There is no greater need today than that of rekindling our torches at the source of light. The final measure of the Church's success is its ability to bear aloft the light that Christ has entrusted to it, the light of a truth that redeems a Protestantism now divided. Our divisions center about the lamp, not about the light. The truth is, we have placed so much emphasis on the lamp that the attention of the world has been diverted from the light. In this we have not only been foolish, we have often been positively sinful. We have made denominational labels the

---

[4] G. Bromley Oxnam, *On This Rock* (New York, Harper & Brothers, 1951), pp. 111, 112. Reprinted by permission of the publishers.

measuring rods of truths which can be realized solely by the acid test of Jesus: "By your fruits, not by your foliage, shall ye be known." What is needed is a Church capable of fulfilling the function of making Christ our sole authority, and his way of life eventually dominant in the lives of men.

We are not saying that belief is unimportant or superfluous. On the contrary we are suggesting a true understanding of vital doctrine, an acknowledgment that it is the Life which is the light of men. If we would face this fact in the spirit of Jesus, the barriers to our fellowship would disappear. They would disappear because we should all agree that they are not big enough to be made issues. "Life is too short to be little," said Disraeli. "The world is my field," said Jesus, and "ye are my witnesses." We must get larger maps! We must find a larger loyalty and thus a more inclusive fellowship, and seriously undertake the redemptive work of Jesus in all the earth.

What is the principal secret of Christianity's power in the world—of its continuity, of its authority, of its endurance and vitality, of its unique capacities for endless self-renewal? It is its possession of Jesus Christ, of the story of His life among men, of the dynamic of his ever-living Presence. All through the nineteen centuries, the portrait of Christ embedded in the Gospels has worked its ever-repeated alchemy—exposing absurdities, restraining excesses, sifting truth from fancy and reality from magic, purifying crude and false notions, rectifying sincere but misguided misinterpretations of himself, stirring imagination, quickening faith, chastening infidelity, winning a devotion ever more intelligent and unalterable. Through those imperfect records, Jesus ever afresh lays constraint upon his Movement in the world, holding it more or less true to his mind and faith, and impelling it to new advances for fulfillment of his purposes. This is the most important single fact about the Christian religion.[5]

[5] Henry P. Van Dusen, *What Is The Church Doing?* (New York, Charles Scribner's Sons, 1943), pp. 156-157. Reprinted by permission of the publishers.

So writes Dr. Henry P. Van Dusen.

From all sides the word comes that the greatest need of the world today is the revival of religion at its best. The present fearful conditions make the witness of the Church more imperative and important than ever before. Into this storm-swept world, the Church must send its message of hope; it must supply the power for both individual salvation and social redemption. We must lay aside the role of the destructive critic and seek to belong to the creative minority.

John, the Baptist, said, "I indeed baptize you with water, but there cometh after me one who will baptize you with the spirit and with fire." We must be the people who are aflame with the fire of God's purpose. When that happens our Christian strategy will be so motivated that it will change the world.

God is working out His purpose. In humble dependence on His divine assistance and in glad loyalty to Him we shall seek to belong to "the fellowship of the concerned." We shall shoulder our responsibility intelligently and joyfully and take our rightful part as active members of a redemptive minority.

> He has sounded forth His trumpet that shall
>   never call retreat;
> He is sifting out the hearts of men before
>   His judgment seat;
> O be swift, my soul, to answer Him, be
>   jubilant my feet;
> Our God is marching on.

No better word can be found with which to conclude this chapter on "The Church of the Future" than those of Nels F. S. Ferré at the end of his truly helpful little book, *Pillars of Faith*:

A new age is here for the receiving of it. It must be built on Eternal Love as the foundation, and held strong and steady on the full five pillars of faith: Jesus Christ, the Holy

Spirit, the Church, the Bible and Christian experiences. If we build in this way, we shall not only believe and work, but believe and work to the fullest possible advantage.[6]

For the questing and hopeful Christian this is a great time in which to live and to bear eloquent witness to the claim "I am a Protestant."

---

[6] Nels F. S. Ferré, *Pillars of Faith* (New York, Harper & Brothers, 1948), p. 125. Reprinted by permission of the publishers.

10

DO YOU BELONG?

THERE is a letter I should like to share with you. It is a very old letter, written some seventeen hundred years ago in Carthage, North Africa, by a Christian leader, Cyprian, to a man named Donatus. A brief word about Cyprian is necessary in order that we may rightly understand and evaluate the letter. Cyprian was one of the outstanding figures in the early Christian Church, the bishop of Carthage from about A.D. 248 until his death in 258. Like the great church leader Tertullian before him, and Augustine who lived later, Cyprian stressed the sovereignty of God and the privilege, responsibility and importance of being a Christian in a pagan world.

Listen to these significant words which Cyprian wrote to Donatus in a letter which is a free translation[1]:

This seems a cheerful world, Donatus, when I view it from this fair garden under the shadow of these vines. But, if I climb some great mountain and look out over the wide lands, you know very well what I would see—brigands on the road, pirates on the high seas, in the amphitheatres men murdering each other to please applauding crowds, under all roofs misery and selfishness. It is really a bad world, Donatus—an incredibly bad world. Yet, in the midst of it, I found a quiet and holy people. They have discovered a joy which is a thousand times better than any pleasure of this sinful life. They are

---

[1] *The Treatises of St. Cyprian* (London, Oxford Press, 1840), in The Library of Holy Catholic Fathers.

213

despised and persecuted—but they care not. These people, Donatus, are the Christians, and I am one of them.

Could you and I write such a letter today? Yes, I am confident we could, at least the first part of it. For that old, old letter is very timely and gives us a most accurate description of the day in which we live. Granted we could easily write the first part, I wonder if you and I who are called Christians could in truth write the latter part and end it with the proud, yet humble claim, "I am one of them." Well, we had better try to write it. What does it mean to belong to the Christian fellowship? Let the late Dr. John Haynes Holmes answer:

It will be agreed that fellowship is the controlling truth of life, the essence alike of morals and religion; and that the maintenance of fellowship is our primary duty. The men of the *Mayflower,* in the famous voyage across the Atlantic, signed a compact binding themselves to stay together when they landed, and not to go wandering off, singly or in small groups, into the wilderness. They did this as an expression of their fidelity to God and to each other, and as the sole means of securing the safety of their community. Fellowship is the sacred word—the golden text of faith. Fellowship is life, and lack of fellowship is death; fellowship is heaven, and lack of fellowship is hell; and the things which we do upon the earth, it is for fellowship's sake that we shall do them.[2]

What does it mean to belong? Many so-called Christians in our time do not really belong to that which gives them the security and strength to live worthily. When I was a student in New York City, I saw Eugene O'Neill's stirring play, *The Hairy Ape.* It made a deep impression on me. It is the story of a stoker on a transatlantic steamship, an unskilled laborer who resembled a "hairy ape" and who failed to find a place in the scheme of things. In sullen defiance, he announces to

_____
[2] By John Haynes Holmes, taken from a church calendar.

the world that "he does not belong." This leads him to a tragic death in the zoo, where he has gone to see if the real hairy ape will provide some of the companionship which he has missed so much. The last scene shows him opening the door of the ape's cage and the ape taking him in his long arms, crushing him and throwing him into a corner of the cage to die. Then we hear this lonely and sullen man cry, "Now I belong." It is not a pleasant picture. Yet many people, as you and I know, gladly give their lives to earthly things, tawdry things, cheap things, to overcome their loneliness and to make them feel they belong. Many feel, like the "Hairy Ape" that they do not belong, and they do not. They are either shut-in or shut-out from the privileges of others.

Yet we, you and I, belong! To what do we belong? That is important to know. As Christians, it is not so important to be serious as it is to be serious about important things. The most important question is: "Can you and I belong to what will make our lives count?" Emerson's wise counsel is helpful: "The lesson of history is to hear what the centuries say against the hours." This lesson of history reveals that far too many belong to the unthinking, dependent and indifferent majority who do not count, while too few belong to the independent, intelligent and saving minority that does.

Do you belong? Do we belong? If we do not, then we are the victims—victims of our own indecision. If we do not find some positive answer, we shall soon cease to be free and hopeful men. Who wants to live in a world devoid of hope? If we do not find honest and hopeful answers to these questions—not quick and easy answers—but honest and hopeful answers, we shall be like the man with one talent who answered when he was accused of not using his talent, "I was afraid and hid it."

The historic evidence is abundant to establish this truth— that the minority is important. At the very dawn of Hebrew history, a leader was pleading with the Judge of all the earth that He should save Sodom from the finality of its iniquities. The Lord said to Abram that He would deliver the city if fifty righteous men could be found in it. The petitioner, realizing that good men were scarce in Sodom, bargained with the Lord as to the requirement and asked that the number be reduced to forty, then thirty, then twenty, and finally he brought the figure down to ten. The Judge of all the earth assured him that if ten good men could be found in the place He would spare it. But they could not be found! Ten righteous men and women will save any city! The world is redeemed not by its majorities but by its righteous minorities.

Through the writings of the major prophets of Israel there runs a constant theme. In passages of exalted vision their hope for the better tomorrow of their people is expressed in the thought of a Redeeming Remnant. This is the dominant theme of the Book of Isaiah from the fortieth chapter onward. The idea is not merely the fanciful dream of an ecstatic prophet. It is one of the actualities of history. Every gain humanity has made has been achieved by a brave, far-seeing, devoted minority.

Jesus stressed this truth in both parable and principle. In the thirteenth chapter of Matthew Jesus was endeavoring to make clear what the Kingdom of God is like. He said it is like

a mustard seed sown in the ground . . . a treasure hidden in the field . . . a householder, who bringeth forth out of his treasure things new and old.

In the thirty-third verse of this thirteenth chapter of Matthew we read:

Another parable spake he unto them; The Kingdom of heaven is like unto leaven, which a woman took, and hid in three measures of meal, till it was all leavened.

We need to consider that parable today and a companion ruling principle found in Matthew 7:13-14, this exhortation:

Enter ye at the strait gate: for wide is the gate, and broad is the way, that leadeth to destruction, and many there be which go in thereat: Because strait is the gate, and narrow the way, which leadeth unto life, and few there be that find it.

In the light of such a parable and of such an exhortation, it is obvious that Jesus did not get his disciples by false pretenses. He told people bluntly what it would cost them if they chose to follow him. With a love of reality, he first faced for himself the fact that the best costs all one has, and then he insisted that candidates for discipleship should do the same. He maintained that it was worth the great cost!

When Jesus began selecting his first disciples from the mass of his countrymen, he was interested not in quantity but quality. He was not thinking primarily of the majority but of the minority. He was interested in that dynamic active leaven (yeast) that, though quantitatively small, nevertheless would be able to transform the whole and make it useful and good. Far from being a matter of sociological and political interest alone, this principle is a central truth of the Judaeo-Christian faith.

Paul, in his letter to the Philippians, called this saving minority, "a colony of heaven." The Philippian Christians would understand that figure of speech, for the city of Philippi was a Roman colony. The Romans were excellent colonizers.

This figure of speech ["a colony of heaven"] carries endless suggestions for the Christian life and task in the modern world.

It suggests the *high adventure* of the Christian enterprise, both in individual *personality* and collective effort—the thrust out into new and unclaimed and unconquered territory. Some

of the most romantic and stirring events of all human history
have been in the founding and development of colonies. Col-
onization is not an armchair job, not a "white-collar job," not
a job for weaklings. Only stout spirits thrive, or even endure,
on a frontier. To think continuously of our task as that of
colonizers will put iron into our blood.[3]

It calls for daring pioneers who will enter into the unredeemed sectors of life and claim them for Christ's dominion.
There is where we, as Christians, too often have failed to be a
"colony of heaven." We may visit some unredeemed area but
we don't settle down and live there and change it.

Charles R. Taft, who, a short time ago, was the President
of the Federal Council of the Churches of Christ in America,
recently said, "The Christian Churches are paying little or no
attention to two thirds of the world." The problems of the
two thirds and our problems cannot be solved just by good
will or sentimental wistful dreaming about the Kingdom of
God. There is no automatic progress. There are successes
and failures. Only under God can we live and move and have
our being. The figure of a "colony of heaven" is one that
identifies those who desire and proclaim the rule and reign of
the highest and the best with God's plan for man.

The early pioneers came to America and established a
theocracy—the rule and reign of God—in their lives. They
came to establish the best they knew of the laws and high
customs of their native land, and to live as free men and
women bound only to God. They believed with Paul that they
were a "colony of heaven," and they stood fast in the freedom
wherewith Christ had set them free.

Is God ashamed of us? Who are the unashamed of God?
That is a pertinent question. God's unashamed are mentioned

---

[3] Halford E. Luccock, *Preaching Values in New Translations of the New
Testament* (New York and Cincinnati, The Abingdon Press, 1928), pp. 297-
298. Reprinted by permission of the publishers.

but once in the Bible. The answer to this question is found in the eleventh chapter of Hebrews—a great chapter which is a roll call of the heroes of the Hebrew faith: "They desire a better country . . . wherefore God is not ashamed of them, to be called their God." Desirers of a better country, they are the "unashamed of God," those who are awake to the possibilities of a better day tomorrow and assume their responsibilities in glad loyalty and consecrated intelligence. It is only as we cease being 4-F's in times of peace that we can make our lives count and become God's unashamed.

We turn to history and find that if we are to count we must belong to the creative minority. Yet many think that our so-called democracy is carried on by the majority.

In consequence, the notion naturally prevails that the majority in the end probably is right and that, anyway, the majority rules. But neither of these ideas is true. The majority is almost certain to be wrong on any matter of fine taste or sound judgment, and, whether or not the majority is right, it certainly does not rule. The dominant influence in every situation is a militant minority. The decision of public policy in this country now is largely determined by resolute, militant, compact, closely organized minorities that want something and get it.[4]

The intelligent minority is aware of the peril of easy formulas; it recalls and relies on the statement of Jeremiah: "Trust not in lying words." The minority, interested in the validity of every issue, need to submit every question to four great moral tests: Is it true? Is it honest? Is it evading responsibility? Is it for the well-being of all humanity? *Minorities are not always right, but every right once began as a minority.* Minorities, therefore, are a necessity and must be protected.

---

[4] Harry Emerson Fosdick, *The Hope of the World* (New York, Harper & Brothers, 1933), p. 2. Reprinted by permission.

The trust of Jesus in the value of the minority is often thwarted because of our worship of bigness. Quality, not quantity, counted with Jesus. Too many of us are not impressed by anything except bigness—big cities, big buildings, big churches, big universities, big corporations. We are all tempted to worship size. But size is utterly a fallacious standard when we are trying to estimate power, usefulness and the things of abiding worth.

There are few things that we Protestant Christians need to learn more exactly than the lesson that bigness does not produce goodness.

Vachel Lindsay has said it well in his poem "On the Building of Springfield"[5]:

> Let not our town be large, remembering
> That little Athens was the Muses' home,
> That Oxford rules the heart of London still,
> That Florence gave the Renaissance to Rome....
>
> Say, is my prophecy too fair and far?
> I only know, unless her faith be high,
> The soul of this, our Nineveh, is doomed,
> Our little Babylon will surely die....
>
> We must have many Lincoln-hearted men.
> A city is not builded in a day.
> And they must do their work, and come and go,
> While countless generations pass away.

Arnold Toynbee has documented the above truth in his *Study of History* and later in *Civilization on Trial.* We must have a righteous minority or perish. The smaller we become geographically, the larger we must become economically, po-

---

[5] Reprinted from *Collected Poems* by Vachel Lindsay, by permission of The Macmillan Company. Copyright 1913, 1914, 1916, 1917, 1919, 1920, 1923 and 1925 by The Macmillan Company.

litically, morally and spiritually, and this is the responsibility of a resolute and righteous minority.

When one thinks of the causes that are on our hearts today—peace rather than war; industrial welfare rather than industrial warfare; good educational opportunities for all the children of this nation and the world—we may well welcome the good news that we do not have to wait for the majority to help others to help themselves. We Christians are to be the saving minority. Jesus declared, "Ye are the salt of the earth . . . Ye are the light of the world . . . Ye are the leaven in the lump."

The Bible is largely the story of the "call" of men to do God's will on the earth. There is Abraham going out to seek a new land "not knowing where he went," finding God and being found of Him. There is Moses hearing God say, "What is that in thine hand?" and being used of God as the great deliverer of his people. There is Amos the herdsman hearing the voice of God amid the lowing of the cattle. There is Isaiah the young priest hearing with bowed head the voice that cried, "Who will go for us?" and answering, "Here am I, send me." There is John the Baptist in the wilderness, with his heart aflame with a fiery passion for righteousness. There are Peter and Andrew, James and John, mending their fishing nets and hearing Jesus say, "Follow me." There is Saul of Tarsus on the road to Damascus, with hate in his heart, finally in humbleness of spirit, saying, in answer to a voice that spoke to him, "Lord, what wilt thou have me to do?" The record of men who have been called of God to do "many mighty works" is found not only in the Book. Wander through the centuries and hear the calling. Is it Luther? Is it Knox? Is it Lincoln? Is it Wilfred Grenfell? Is it Albert Schweitzer? Or is it the multitude of others, inconspicuous or undistinguished, who have made their witness and "kept the faith?" *You* answer!

This we know, it is a truth well established; it is a truth we do well to underline: *Christian men and women, one by one, count for much*. But besides good hearts, they must have good heads, *real* tough-mindedness, willing hands and the purpose of God as their goal.

A few years ago I visited Boulder Dam, now named Hoover Dam. There I read on a plaque a beautiful line: "They died that the desert might bloom." This was the story of 89 men who had perished in completing the great engineering feat. Four reasons were given: clear vision, careful planning, hard work and worthy sacrifice. So it is with social engineering. We have achieved the place in the world where the claim "as goes America, so goes the world" has validity because we have observed those principles and have rightly combined the dignity of thought with the dignity of work. Henri Bergson, the philosopher, has well stated a sound principle of life: "that we shall think like men of action and act like men of thought." Bonaro Overstreet has also shown the value of a man's efforts:

> You say that the little efforts that I make
> Will do no good;
> They never will prevail
> To tip the hovering scale
> Where justice hangs in balance.
> I don't think
> I ever thought they would,
> But I am prejudiced beyond debate
> In favor of my right to choose which side
> Shall feel the stubborn ounces of my weight.[6]

The individual counts if he puts the stubborn ounces of his weight with others and forms a minority to do God's will. "Individual greatness is no match for humble togetherness."

---

[6] Bonaro Overstreet, "To One Who Doubts the Worth of Doing Anything If You Can't Do Everything." Reprinted by permission of the author.

But even "togetherness" is not enough. Something else is needed to make our Christian faith meaningful today. It is the ability to acknowledge Jesus as Master, the ability to place self-imposed discipline upon one's self.

Protestant Christianity will remain strong and increase in strength and virility only as disciplines are self-imposed by the Christian and the Church. These disciplines include prayer and the use of money and all the areas of life. Christian discipleship requires discipline.

William James reminded us again and again that character is strengthened by the discipline of doing worth-while things. Life is not easy. Paul knew this, and points the way to self-mastery and victory over life: "Put on the Lord Jesus Christ and make no provision for the flesh." How can we "put on the Lord Jesus Christ"? The following is a discipline for Christian living:

1. Attend church regularly and practice the presence of God daily—without exception.

2. Read one chapter of the Bible each day, beginning with the New Testament, Matthew 1.

3. Approach all men and situations (good or evil) with a Christian attitude of sympathetic understanding, appreciation and positive helpfulness.

4. Strive for a will-to-believe that "all things work together for good to them that love God."

5. Pursue as the dominant ambition and purpose of life, the attainment of "oneness with God in Christ" and the peace, strength, and quality of soul that flow from it.

6. Believe in and seek community with "The Holy Catholic Church"—"the body of Christ."

7. Bear witness to the peace and power of God in the daily routine of life, through radiant living, marked by a spirit of joy and thanks-giving.[7]

---

[7] Commission on Evangelism of the Evangelic Reformed Church, 2969 West 25th Street, Cleveland 13, Ohio.

This is the plan advocated by the Evangelical and Reformed Church. It illustrates the attempt to aid its members in spiritual growth through self-imposed discipline.

Only those people who are disciplined for the sake of their cause will succeed in filling its demand. Disciplines imposed on the Communists have made them a group to reckon with. Self-imposed disciplines made by the Christians will help us to know that ours is not a theology to defend but a gospel to claim, and make it the greatest force—for good—in all the world. Only disciplined power is effective power.

Of all the titles given to Jesus, or those which he in self designation, gave to himself, none is more needed than that of "Master." To be sure, the word *Master* is not accepted by many. To them it means serfdom and servility. Yet, appreciative of this point of view as we are, we need to know that all of us need a Master, in the best and fullest use of the word.

Man must be master over himself. That is a great thing to achieve through the help and power of God. But the last and the greatest need of man is what? We answer: not to be a master, but to be mastered by something—yes, by someone higher and better than himself, even by God through Christ. *Not something to serve but something which we ourselves may properly serve. Something, yes, Someone who is great enough and good enough to command our glad loyalty, organize us, unify us and so call forth all the latent energies of our lives, that we may be enabled to concentrate on the great task of living life worthily according to the plan and purpose of God.*

"The great hours are those when some bondage is broken," wrote Nietzsche. Yet the greatest hours are those not when some limiting bond is broken, but when some empowering bondage is assumed—when we are imprisoned by the best. The Christian is one who enlists in Christ's cause. Then he is captured by the message, the life and the spirit of him who came to bring us into bondage to God, in order to make us free and "prisoners of hope."

The highroad of self-realization is always by the narrow road of self-mastery. It is hard to be a Christian. (Jesus did not come to make life easy; he came to make men great.) One needs Someone whom he can trust to help him to stand up to life and carry on to a worthy conclusion.

We cannot limit Christ and truly belong to his fellowship. As Dr. Bosley has well said:

Christ limited is Christ betrayed—this is tragically true. And it is gloriously true that Christ unlimited is Christ fulfilled and in that fulfillment men find salvation. He is the Lord of life—not just this piece or that fragment of life, but the whole of it. So to see him, so to believe him, so to worship him, so to present him to the world in which we live—this is the Christian gospel and the Christian mission.[8]

You and I can never be free, or really live, unless we are mastered. You and I can never be master over ourselves, master over the various and perplexing circumstances of life, and master over others—to their own well-being—unless you and I are mastered by the Master of men! You and I need a Master, the Master, even Christ. Then you and I can climb some hill and, looking out over this pagan world, can, with Cyprian of old, not only write the first part of the letter about the world's woes, but finish it as he did, believing one also has his life's answer when one says, "I am one of them." I am one of the Christians! I am leaven! I belong! Belong both to man and to God! I am one of God's unashamed. I have shouldered my responsibility.

Now is no time to cry with Hamlet: "The time is out of joint: O cursed spite, that ever I was born to set it right."

[8] Harold A. Bosley, "Christ Limited Is Christ Betrayed." Reprinted by permission of *The Pulpit* from the issue of February 1951.

Every age is momentous; our age is climactic. It is a great time in which to live if we can say with Rupert Brooke: "Now God be thanked who has matched us with this hour!" This is our privilege as Protestants: trusting in God and with a deep and unshaken loyalty to His will, as revealed in Jesus Christ, you and I can belong to the fellowship of believers. You and I can make our witness by word and life to the Gospel, the "good news" of the redemptive judgment and love of God. In true humility, honest appreciation and eager expectancy may each of us say: "I am a Protestant."

SUGGESTED ADDITIONAL READING
AND INDEX

SUGGESTED ADDITIONAL READING

Preparation of a volume such as *I Am a Protestant* requires the reading of hundreds of books on the subject. Many of these are too technical or otherwise lacking in interest for the average layman. But, for the reader who cares to do a little more reading in the field of Protestantism, I have selected fifteen titles, which I recommend heartily:

Bainton, Roland Herbert, *Here I Stand, A Life of Martin Luther*.
Abingdon-Cokesbury Press, 1950.
Coffin, Henry Sloane, *God Confronts Man in History*.
Charles Scribner's Sons, 1947.
Ferré, Nels F. S., *Pillars of Faith*.
Harper and Brothers, 1948.
Fosdick, Harry Emerson, *The Man from Nazareth*.
Harper and Brothers, 1950.
Goodspeed, Edgar J., *The Life of Christ*.
Harper and Brothers, 1950.
Leber, Charles Tudor, (ed.), *World Faith in Action*.
The Bobbs-Merrill Company, Inc., 1951.
Morrison, Charles Clayton, *Can Protestantism Win America?*
Harper and Brothers, 1948.
Nichols, James Hastings, *Primer for Protestants*.
Association Press, 1947.
Oxnam, B. Bromley, *On This Rock*.
Harper and Brothers, 1951.
Richardson, Cyril Charles, *The Church Through the Centuries*.
Charles Scribner's Sons, 1938.

Sherrill, Henry Knox, *The Church's Ministry in Our Time.*
    Charles Scribner's Sons, 1949.
Van Dusen, Henry Pitney, *What Is the Church Doing?*
    Charles Scribner's Sons, 1943.
Walker, Williston, *The Great Men of the Christian Church.*
    The University of Chicago Press, 1908.
Walker, Williston, *A History of the Christian Church.*
    Charles Scribner's Sons, 1918.
Williams, Daniel Day, *God's Grace and Man's Hope.*
    Harper and Brothers, 1949.

INDEX

284
J54

DATE DUE

MAR 4 '86			
	Lincoln Christian College		
GAYLORD			PRINTED IN U.S.A.